PRAISE FOR *THE JOYFUL LEADER*

"*The Joyful Leader* is exactly the book you need if you're feeling the burn of the corporate grind. This book goes beyond talking about resilience—it's packed with actionable steps that help you tap into joy, tackle stress, and bounce back stronger than ever. For anyone looking to rekindle their work passion or find their footing amidst challenges, this guide is your go-to for transforming pressure into performance. Dive in and let it inspire you to lead with resilience and joy!"

~Aria Johnson
TV Personality

"Nicole Van Valen is a past colleague and friend whose input I greatly value. She's an expert in navigating organizational culture. Her expertise that she shares in *The Joyful Leader* is an invaluable resource for leaders looking to navigate success within company cultures."

~Taft Parsons III
Chief Psychiatric Officer of CVS Health

"In all my years as an executive, there has been no topic timelier than resilience. Resilience in our work and personal lives is key to meeting today's challenges. *The Joyful Leader* offers practical advice and tools through examples and stories that help you create your process for resilience and joy in your life. This is a must-read!"

~**Kelvin McLaurin, CPA**
Partner at MJK Solutions
Former SVP of Global Business Services at
McDonald's Corporation and CVS Health

"*The Joyful Leader* is ahead of its time. Learning about why and how people push themselves to be better can be mythical—until you read Nicole Van Valen's work. We all have a spirit of can-do and will-do."

~**Dr. Thomas RaShad Easley**
Founder of Mind Heart for Diversity Consulting
Former Inaugural Assistant Dean of Community and
Inclusion at the School of the Environment at
Yale University

"*The Joyful Leader* is a must-read for anyone feeling the weight of corporate burnout. It offers practical steps to transform workplace challenges into opportunities for growth and joy. This book empowers readers to take control of their careers with renewed resilience and purpose."

~**John "JR" Register, CSP and PLY**
Top 50 Global Keynote Speaker and Author
Paralympic Silver Medalist, USA Track and Field
Combat Veteran

"Nicole Van Valen is a sharp, brilliant mind with so much to teach us all. I am inspired by the gifts she has to share in *The Joyful Leader* with anyone looking to shift their life towards joy."

~Beanie Feldstein
Actor

"This book just might be the most important book of this decade. With compelling studies and interesting stories, *The Joyful Leader* has profound insights on how to enhance our lives. This gem is a joy to read."

~Pedrya Seymour
Two-Time Olympian, Bahamas Track and Field

"This book is a beacon of hope and practical wisdom. As an entrepreneur and keynote speaker focused on transformation and leadership, I've seen firsthand the impact of stress on business success. Nicole Van Valen's *The Joyful Leader* is an essential guide for anyone looking to turn challenges into opportunities through resilience and joy. This book offers powerful strategies that will help you reclaim control of your career and elevate your leadership, making it a must-read for professionals at all levels."

~Danny Goldberg
Award-Winning Entrepreneur
Workplace Care Expert

"This insightful book is an essential read for anyone feeling trapped by the demands of the modern workplace. With a powerful blend of practical advice and inspiring stories, *The Joyful Leader* illuminates a path to self-discovery and resilience, empowering you to transform challenges into opportunities for growth and fulfillment. Get ready to embrace the journey: Ready, Set, Go!"

~Mercedes Martin
CEO and Founder of Mercedes Martin & Company

"*The Joyful Leader* is a must-read for anyone looking to infuse joy into their work life. Nicole will take you step by step on an actionable journey toward discovering your own limitless power to create a more resilient, joyful, and successful you!"

~Karélix Alicea, MS, BCBA, ITDS
Founder and President of Lotus Behavioral Interventions
Intensive Practicum Supervisor for
Simmons College, FIT and USF
Former Miami HEAT Dancer and Former Actor

"In *The Joyful Leader*, Nicole Van Valen's approach of fostering resilience through the cultivation of a boundless reservoir of inner resources delivers a transformative experience. She brings a wealth of knowledge and skill on how to cultivate a growth mindset and transform personal challenges into stepping stones for achievement. Collaborating with Nicole is always inspiring. Her vibrant joy and profound passion infuse every interaction with energy and possibility."

~Liza Rossi
Founder of Ekukhanyeni Relief Project
Cofounder of Love Energy Techniques
Diplomat Representing South Africa under President
Nelson Mandela

"Nicole Van Valen's *The Joyful Leader* is a transformative guide that beautifully blends deep insight with practical strategies for cultivating resilience and joy. After my conversation with Nicole, I found myself reflecting more on my own journey and path to resilience. This book is a must-read for anyone looking to reclaim their energy and purpose in both life and work."

~Robyn Hatcher
Certified Professional Speaker | Consultant
Author and Actor
Former Writer for *All My Children* and *One Life to Live*

"In a world where burnout and stress dominate the workplace, Nicole Van Valen's *The Joyful Leader* is a breath of fresh air. It offers a powerful roadmap to reclaiming energy, purpose, and joy, both personally and professionally. Nicole's unique three-stage model—Ready, Set, Go—provides actionable strategies that resonate deeply. This isn't just another self-help book; it's a transformative guide that empowers readers to cultivate resilience from within and navigate the complexities of modern work life with renewed strength and enthusiasm. If you're ready to take control of your career and well-being, this book is your essential companion."

~Naya Tapper
Two-Time Olympian, Bronze Medalist, USA Rugby

"Nicole Van Valen's *The Joyful Leader* really hit home for me. Having experienced both the excitement and stress of the NFL cheerleading world, and now balancing a global event planning career, resilience is something I've had to build over time. Nicole's approach of finding joy in the midst of adversity is so relatable, and I believe this book will inspire anyone looking to lead with heart and strength."

~Bailey Brooks Mashburn
CEO of How 2 Wed
Executive Director of Kennedy Kids
Former Miami Dolphins Cheerleader

"The essence of this book is revealed from the beginning: 'This roadmap does not shy away from the hard truths or avoid the complexities of leadership. Instead, it equips you with the tools you need to navigate challenges effectively, ensuring you can lead with confidence.' From that point onward, *The Joyful Leader* fulfills its promise. If you pay attention, accept those hard truths, and take what Nicole Van Valen says to heart, you will be a different leader when you are done reading her book."

~Bruce Turkel
Author of *All About Them*

THE JOYFUL
LEADER

THE JOYFUL LEADER

Discover Resilience Through Joy and Manage Stress to Elevate Your Leadership and Organizational Culture

NICOLE VAN VALEN, MS, LMFT, SHRM-SCP

For permission requests, write to the publisher, addressed "Attention: Permissions Coordinator," at the address below.

Publish Your Purpose
141 Weston Street, #155
Hartford, CT, 06141

PYP **Publish**
Your Purpose

The opinions expressed by the Author are not necessarily those held by Publish Your Purpose.

Ordering Information: Quantity sales and special discounts are available on quantity purchases by corporations, associations, and others. For details, contact the author at information@keaneinsights.com.

For more about the author, upcoming events, and additional resources, visit keaneinsights.com or follow on LinkedIn: linkedin.com/in/nicolevanvalen and linkedin.com/company/keane-insights

Edited by: Nancy Graham-Tillman & Carlee Jeanne Frank
Cover design by: Nelly Murariu
Typeset and e-book design by: Amit Dey

ISBN: 979-8-88797-152-0 (hardcover)
ISBN: 979-8-88797-153-7 (paperback)
ISBN: 979-8-88797-154-4 (ebook)

Library of Congress Control Number: 2024949088

First edition, January 2026.

Do you have a book idea you would like us to consider publishing? Please visit PublishYourPurpose.com for more information.

DEDICATION

With profound gratitude and heartfelt appreciation, I dedicate this book to you, the reader. You have sacrificed much as an intrapreneur or entrepreneur and come to understand that success at work and joy in life can coexist. Thank you for believing in and caring for yourself by pursuing and expanding what brings you joy.

As Rocky Balboa once said, "Every champion was once a contender who refused to give up."[1] This quote embodies my journey and the resilience I wish to impart to you, dear reader. May this book inspire you to maintain your energy, make wise decisions for self-care, and positively impact the world while meeting your goals in harmony.

---

[1] *Rocky Balboa*, directed by Sylvester Stallone (2006, United States: Sony Pictures Home Entertainment, 2007), DVD.

NOTICE TO READERS

This book addresses topics related to mental health, including discussions of stress, anxiety, depression, and other sensitive issues. Some readers may find these topics triggering or emotionally challenging. Please prioritize your well-being as you engage with this content. If you find yourself feeling overwhelmed or in need of support, we encourage you to reach out to a trusted mental health professional or helpline in your area. You are not alone, and help is available.

CONTENTS

FOREWORD

Are you looking to transform your life? Do you constantly feel tired, lack energy, and dread getting out of bed? Are you fearful of or do you despise going into the office? Unfortunately, so many people feel this way, which is truly a sad situation. I am here to tell you that you do not have to feel this way! What you are about to read will help you transform your life so that you feel much more energy and positivity. You will be ready and eager to take on the day, ready to go to work, and not just survive but thrive. Most importantly, this book will help you create an unbreakable mindset to succeed through challenging times in your life.

Look, we all have to deal with stress and challenging times in our lives, but challenging times do not mean impossible times! *The Joyful Leader* is the perfect book to help you develop and sustain a resilient mindset through focusing on creating joy in your life. When we are in a state of joy, we learn how to manage stress much more effectively, which allows us to live and lead a more purpose-driven life. This book gives you essential tools needed to thrive in uncertain and challenging times when they arise in our lives! It will change your life for the better and allow you to start living life on your own terms.

I write this forward with the highest regard for Nicole Van Valen and this amazing book! You are about to embark on a journey to create purpose, prosperity, and greatness in your life. Enjoy the ride!

MARQUES OGDEN

Founder and CEO of Ogden Ventures
National and International Keynote Speaker
Business Coach, Corporate Consultant, Brand Ambassador, and Podcast Host
Four-Time Best-Selling Author
Former NFL Athlete

Marques Ogden is on a mission to inspire the masses to maximize their potential to reach their personal and professional goals.

DEAR READER

What's the best dance to pair with chips?
Salsa!

~Emily Strickland, "15 Corny Dance Jokes to
Brighten Your Day"

As a former Miami Dolphins Cheerleader and Miami HEAT Dancer, I got nervous before every performance. I'd start thinking, *That's a big crowd out there. Will I remember all the choreography?* As I'd wait for the announcer to call our name and introduce us onto the court or field, my adrenaline would start pumping. Once "The Heat Is On" started playing, my stress level heightened, my chest tightened, a lump formed in my throat, and my mouth felt dry.

However, when I got onto that field or court and heard the music, I began performing, dancing my way onto the stage. I could feel the positive energy of the crowd in the stadium or arena, and my nervous energy turned into sheer joy. I go

through that same experience each time I get on stage to deliver a speech.

Performing under stress became a common experience for me, not only in the entertainment world but also in the corporate arena. I've been through so many organizational changes, from acquisitions and mergers to department reorganizations and leadership and team changes. I've been in health care for over 25 years (no, I'm not going to tell you my age), and through them all, my experiences have ignited my passion to help people grow their resilience so they can deal with change.

I hold several degrees and have spent a lot of time studying families and organizations, and what has helped me the most is family therapy and working with clients. This is where I started to see the dynamics of people and understand the stresses of relationships. But I'm not here to tell you about how great I am, because we're all pretty great. I'm here to share with you that through all that education and navigation of the corporate world, I realized that I've been stressed nearly half of my life. And I didn't even know I was unhappy.

Initially, I thought I would find my resilience at work. I thought it was my manager's responsibility to make my life easier and help me get promoted. I also believed that my coworkers would be like a family who'd lift each other up. But many times, I found myself in a one-sided relationship, one in which I was not taken care of.

Being the people-pleaser and hyper-achiever that I was, I became a workaholic—yet nothing changed. In fact, when my daughter was younger, she thought I never went to sleep. I'd put her to bed at night and then get on the computer, and I'd still be on the computer when it was time to wake her up. I was always at that computer before everyone got up. I didn't realize I was in a toxic environment with a toxic manager and not-so-friendly coworkers.

I dealt with the stress by working even harder. Maybe for some of you, you deal with stress by turning to two glasses of wine instead of one or eating the whole pizza instead of your usual two slices. Though there will always be stressors in our lives, I've learned over time, and I'm still learning that being resilient is our own individual responsibility. For me, I turn to what I enjoy and use dance as a de-stressor.

A rubber band that is pulled too tight will eventually snap back into shape. I want you to be the rubber band. I've seen it all and have experienced a great deal of it myself. After working with thousands of people in stressful situations, I've found that there's a pattern with everyone and that resilient people do three main things, and those are what I've built my formula on.

I know firsthand that growing your resilience is critical for your career growth, because I've been there. For me, my highest level of stress occurred during the time when I had to drive one hour to and from home each day to take my daughter to dance classes, adjusting to being on a new team at work with increased deadlines but without direction, and working from home with a lack of work–life balance. Throughout my career, however, dance was my safety net. It was an important part of my life because it was the stress release I needed to find my resilience. That resilience guided me as I navigated the corporate world, and we all know how stressful that can be at times—from getting acclimated to a new role, adjusting to a new workplace culture, working with a new manager, dealing with difficult coworkers, and fearing layoffs.

When we allow stress to take over, and if we don't use any sort of plan to grow our resilience, it can lead us to higher levels of distress under pressure and hopelessness in the face of difficulty, worry, and fatigue. On top of that, sleep disruption leads to higher employee turnover rates, increased workloads, and loss of productivity.

I'm here to help you be the rubber band. I can't overexaggerate the importance of growing your resilience. Together, we're going to explore how to use stress to grow resilience, because doing so has helped me beyond measure, and I want the same for you.

It's no secret that as an upper-level business professional or entrepreneur, you're experiencing burnout. You're living a fast-paced lifestyle and likely believe you don't have enough time for joy or feel guilty about doing enjoyable things. Perhaps you know you're feeling stressed but don't know how to find joy in your life, and you've been mistaking your work as your sole source of joy. Maybe you're at the point where you're engaging in avoidance, negative self-talk, and micromanagement, all of which are trapping you in isolation. To alleviate your stress, perhaps you've been engaging in unhealthy coping mechanisms such as overworking, using or abusing substances, consuming too much junk food, sleeping too much, and not exercising.

You're not alone. Burnout is real, and it can lead to serious consequences both personally and professionally. If you've finally realized that your lifestyle is not only unsustainable but is actually exacerbating your stress and reducing your productivity, you've come to the right place. You're now in a safe space to find your joy and take time for self-care. You don't have to know all the answers, you don't have to be perfect, and you're in good company with your desire to improve your personal and professional life. It's okay to be open and vulnerable with yourself in this quiet space of self-reflection so that you can then emerge full of hope and joy, with the energy to be your professionally authentic self.

This book is an enlightening guide that encompasses a systemic model for addressing the multilayered challenges you're facing as an upper-level manager or executive. In this safe space, I will help you focus on improving your productivity and your business profitability while also empowering your leaders to enhance their well-being and mental health. I will guide you towards discovering yourself, designing your landscape, and delivering on your goals by offering you a roadmap to self-discovery.

The roadmap is a continuous cycle, a Sphere of Resilience, as you'll soon see. As we become lifelong learners, growing and expanding our knowledge and experiences, we are transformed into higher levels of ourselves and begin to see life differently and more profoundly. Sometimes this happens when we meet someone who enhances our way of thinking, just as it did for me.

I remember sitting at a preconference session where Nido Qubein, President of High Point University in North Carolina and founder and Chairperson Emeritus of the National Speakers Association Foundation, encouraged us to pay attention to the way people think. I embraced his advice, which transformed my perspective during the conference as well as in my post-conference reflections. At the preconference session, I was also captivated by Marc Randolph, cofounder of Netflix, who shared his journey of starting and sustaining the company. Randolph's insights on failure were particularly enlightening.

He views everything as an experiment driven by curiosity, and that deeply resonated with me. His approach confirmed my passion for resilience and helping others overcome barriers, and his perspective reinforced my belief that thinking differently can lead to success and is a crucial differentiator.

I believe I was placed here to inspire others to find their resilience and discover better ways to reach their goals. Randolph's encouragement to never give up and let curiosity drive me was profoundly motivating. It all starts with experimenting, not striving for perfection. Curiosity can indeed lead the way to resilience.

Through these pages, I'm giving you permission to get curious and do something only for yourself, and I'm offering a space to be free and the time to enjoy being you—uninterrupted. As you read, you get to focus on yourself by minding your own business and freeing yourself from all the noise and chaos of others and the world. I want you to feel refreshed from being immersed in joyful activities.

While this roadmap offers actionable steps, it does not provide quick fixes or frivolous, superficial solutions. Instead, it aims to inspire and motivate you with real-life examples and practical strategies that build insight, awareness, and skill. The goal is to help you achieve a place of joy and fulfillment in all areas of your life by understanding the benefits of discovering your joy. I want to motivate you to practice preventative joyful activities so that you not only feel less stressed and avoid burnout but have the means to be prepared and energized so you can cope with the changes and challenges you're facing and will face.

The roadmap in this book provides insights on ways to meet your goals more efficiently—and with less emotional xxx | The Joyful Leader

havoc—through developing a growth mindset that allows you to act, engage, and succeed. As I help guide you through evaluations, analyses, and strategies for continuous improvement, you will learn by doing, engaging, and succeeding. Together, we will discover *you*, both personally and professionally.

This roadmap does not shy away from the hard truths or avoid the complexities of leadership. Instead, it equips you with the tools you need to navigate challenges effectively, ensuring you can lead with confidence and resilience. At the end of the journey, you will feel different, think differently, and see challenges in a new light. Your interactions with others will be positively impacted, and in turn you'll have a positive ripple effect on your relationships and networks as you influence your environment. You will have a sense of control over your thoughts and behaviors and a more positive outlook on life. As you move towards achieving your goals, you will gain more self-confidence, which will help you continue to grow and succeed. You'll have a clearer understanding of how to balance the demands of your professional role with your personal well-being, fostering a more sustainable and fulfilling approach to leadership.

As leaders, we must prioritize our own mental health and well-being so that we can create environments where individuals feel safe and supported under our leadership. It's crucial to find joy in life because it significantly enhances our overall wellness. By exercising resilience in both personal and professional settings, we can redesign our lives to achieve our goals and thrive, allowing us to navigate stress and find joy in the journey.

Let's get started.

THE SYMBOLISM OF THE PHOENIX: RISING TO LEAD WITH RESILIENCE

The cover image for *The Joyful Leader* was chosen with deep intent. The phoenix is a legendary bird known for its cycle of rebirth, which encapsulates the essence of resilience and leadership. It symbolizes the unwavering spirit that rises stronger and more vibrant after facing the fires of challenge and transformation. This is the journey of a leader—to not only withstand adversity but grow through it.

The phoenix on the cover is not just visually striking but rich with meaning through purposeful color representation[2]. The phoenix is always golden, representing the innate value and essence each of us carries within. Its wings depict the experiences of life that guide us towards enlightenment through different shades:

- The Phoenix is gold because it is a reminder of the inherent potential and purity we possess.

---

[2] Liza Rossi, "How to Teach: SEC Cleansing & Merkaba Activators Recordings - Step 1," Love Energy Techniques, January 6–8, 2024, Lucca, Italy, Villa Il Tiglio, unpublished presentation.

- Red symbolizes those moments of rage and intense emotion that often signal the start of significant challenges.

- Orange reflects anger that when harnessed with awareness fuels powerful change and growth.

- Yellow brings both unhappiness and the warmth of happiness, a reminder to embrace the present as a stepping stone to a brighter future.

- Green represents renewal and the steady nurturing of sustaining joy, which is required to thrive even amid trials.

- Blue embodies bliss, the deep contentment that comes from overcoming obstacles and aligning with our true purpose.

- Purple marks the ultimate stage of transcendence and profound insight, symbolizing the wisdom gained through our experiences.

- Black in the background signifies the love that supports resilience and allows us to rise with compassion and understanding.

Throughout each stage, the phoenix remains unwavering, embodying the journey of resilience that repeats with each new challenge or change. These cycles mirror the three stages of resilience detailed in this book: (1) rediscovering yourself as you reconnect with your core values and strengths, (2) redesigning your landscape by building connections, environments, and support networks that align with your evolved self, and (3) delivering on your goals as you rise equipped with lessons learned and ready to make an impactful difference.

As you read *The Joyful Leader*, I encourage you to see yourself in this phoenix. Recognize your own golden essence, value each color of experience, and rise stronger and more prepared to lead with joy and resilience. This book is your guide to not only facing challenges but transforming them into your greatest achievements. Remember, like the phoenix, each trial may leave behind ashes, but it is from those ashes that you will emerge with renewed purpose, ready to shine golden once more.

PART 1

THE FOUNDATION

Does this sound like you?

- Slacking at work
- Calling in sick more often
- Dreading going to work
- Having trouble concentrating
- Engaging in negative self-talk
- Considering quitting your job or being close to losing your job
- Running continuously on a hamster wheel every day, feeling completely exhausted yet not getting anywhere
- Being unable to function at all

Without resilience, a build-up of stressful experiences can make us feel like we're about to burst like a balloon. When the balloon pops, it means we're at the point of burnout.

There is a way to overcome stress and burnout and to grow and preserve your energy. And it's not necessarily leaving your job. After all, sometimes even when we want to leave, we can't. If you're in a toxic environment that you can't leave right away, you need a strategy to remain safe, much like being in a domestic violence situation.

That strategy is just within your reach. It's a part of you that has always been there. It's a part of your essence and is what makes you unique. This strategy is a loving and nurturing pathway to happiness and joy, and even to bliss and beyond. But it's a road less traveled because we forgot the way, thinking we don't have time for it, or believing it won't really get us anywhere. Yet we need it to survive and thrive.

The way out of falling victim to workplace stress and burnout is building resilience through joy by discovering yourself, influencing your environment, and meeting your goals. Through insights, stories, and calls-to-action, you will come to understand the importance of joy, the impact of stress, and the power of resilience. It is at this intersection that resilience, mental wellness, and productivity come together, with joy at the center.

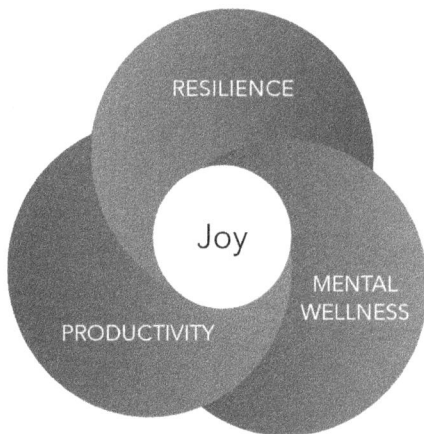

The Power of Joy™

Let's explore why joy matters. Then we'll move into how stress keeps us from joy and how we can use that stress to find joy again and ultimately become more resilient and productive.

CHAPTER 1

TAPPING INTO JOY

> *How many tickles does it take to make an*
> *octopus laugh?*
> *Ten-tickles!*
>
> ~John Brueckner, *World's Greatest Dad Jokes*

You deserve to be happy, even joyful.

You spend a large portion of your day at work putting your best effort into what you do, ultimately providing great value to all those who encounter you. But when was the last time you were really happy, let alone joyful?

Joy is a big deal. Some of you may be rolling your eyes, thinking that talking about joy is just fluff, especially in the workplace. Yet when you go to work and see a miserable person and look at their performance and how they lead their teams, can there be any doubt that joy really does matter? And how many of us have walked into a store and been impacted by someone's attitude on the other side of the counter? In terms of joy, the biggest perspective shift we can make is to see joy as a must-have rather than a nice-to-have.

Many of us have been taught to put ourselves last, to the point of it being ingrained in us to always be doing for others. Maybe doing something for yourself is a new concept to you. I need you to know that it's not only okay to do something for yourself but essential.

When we're joyful, we feel like ourselves—our true, authentic selves—and others can see our essence, the core of who we are as individuals. For example, I've always been known to have uncontrollable laughter. People who know me know that if I find something funny, it takes a while for me to stop laughing. Humor has always been a way for me to connect with people, and one of the things that brings me joy is dad jokes. And you know what I did? I brought "dad jokes" into my corporate meetings. I'd start my meetings with a joke, even when those meetings included senior leadership team members (of course, I'd tie the joke into that day's discussion). It lightened the room and shifted people's minds, especially during brainstorming sessions. People were able to loosen up and laugh a little before getting into the heavy stuff.

Embracing joy through using humor created a level of unspoken trust because we all started our time together with a laugh. It loosened people up and gave them an opportunity to relax and be themselves. The atmosphere became friendly, and we were all on the same page. Sometimes I told the joke all wrong, but people still laughed simply because I usually started with my infectious laugh before I even finished the joke. And when a snort was involved in the laughter, that's how you knew it was really funny. What a way to bond with a team!

WHY JOY MATTERS

Joy is an experience anyone can feel. When we're authentically ourselves, we find joy more easily, and finding joy leads to resilience. Yes, even in the workplace. Workplace mental wellness matters. It matters because bringing our best self to the job is how we remain resilient and, in turn, productive.

I was once asked what is the difference between happiness and joy. The difference is subtle yet profound. Research notes that happiness is a fleeting emotion tied to external events and immediate gratification, while joy is a deeper, more enduring state rooted in internal fulfillment and resilience.[1] I spoke with Liza Rossi, founder of Ekukhanyeni Relief Project, cofounder of Love Energy Techniques, and former diplomat for the Department of Internal Relations and Cooperations of South Africa under President Nelson Mandela. She insightfully added that "Happiness is more of a static kind of emotion or state of being. But joy is actually accessing different parts of yourself and higher levels of yourself to bring you into that state of joy." Joy transcends immediate circumstances, connecting us with a deeper sense of purpose and self-awareness.

The challenge for many lies in moving beyond surface-level happiness to tap into the more fulfilling state of joy, especially when the tools to access it aren't readily available. Many people struggle to differentiate between the two, particularly when it comes to finding joy outside of work. After I gave a keynote speech about resilience, for instance, a cofounder of a small marketing business asked me if my joy is in developing and working on strategies for companies like hers. She seemed to be having a difficult time figuring out what her joy was outside of work and was looking for answers. Many others have the same difficulty. Curious about how others navigate this challenge, I decided to explore further.

My business Keane Insights™, which is dedicated to empowering leaders and organizations through resilience and strategic development, conducted a survey about the impact of joyful activities on work. We asked participants, "What activities bring you the most joy and help you stay resilient at work?" Of the total number of participants, 40% said that social interactions bring them the most joy, followed by mindfulness and relaxation at 30%. Physical exercise and creative hobbies also play significant roles. We then asked participants the follow-up question, "How do joyful activities outside of work impact your performance and resilience at work?" A whopping 67% said joyful activities outside of work significantly improve their performance and resilience at work. Furthermore, when we asked the question, "How do you measure the impact of joy on workplace productivity?" 65% said observing team morale and engagement is key. This answer highlights the less tangible but vital aspects of workplace joy.

Clearly, what we do off the clock deeply impacts our work life. Identifying challenges is the first step towards the path to joy and beyond. This poll allowed people to become introspective, understand their challenges and personal resilience, and change the way they think about joy in their lives. It opened discussions between me and business executives about their thoughts on the importance of finding joy and resilience and its impact on their professional lives. Some shared personal experiences, such as how their love of music and getting out to live shows has been their favorite way to recharge. This is a dialogue that doesn't happen often and seems like a novel idea to many. It's amazing when we find simple things we can do that uplift us to a more joyful state of mind so we can balance any stressors in our lives.

My wish is for people to discover more joy and beyond in their lives. When people are supported in engaging well-being practices to enhance their personal joy and resilience, especially by their employers, this healthy combination becomes the secret sauce for success. Creating joy in the workplace is essential and should not just be observed but measured, because joyful activities have a significant return on investment. As Rossi wisely remarked, "It's what you don't see, what you can't measure, that is the most important. A person who is working in joy and is resilient and authentic can bring about a superb program. If you're truly using the energies of joy to create something, how can it not be successful?"

While measuring joy may be challenging, its impact on success is undeniable, making it a critical element to cultivate and assess in any workplace. One way to measure the impact of joy is by tracking our productivity and performance metrics. One powerful tool for this is Keane Insights' three-step model for assessing your resilience, which starts with discovering your joy.

DISCOVERING JOY

Finding joy is a vital step on the path to resilience, but in living our high-stress lives, joy often takes a back seat. Even in—and perhaps especially during—highly stressful situations, the most resilient people find a way to incorporate joy into their lives.

One of my favorite parts of the work I do is getting to talk to so many fascinating people who have persevered through so much to ultimately become not only highly successful but joyful. In turn, they radiate joy for others and inspire them to find joy in their own lives. One such person is Nikki Spoelstra, former Miami HEAT Dancer and now host of the top-rated podcast *The Know with Nikki Spo*. Her podcast is a safe space where she inspires women by sharing stories of perseverance and hope, and Spoelstra works to amplify other women's voices by, in her words, "helping them honor their inner knowing and live their most authentic lives."

Spoelstra and I have stayed in touch ever since I was her assistant director at Miami HEAT, and I sat down to interview her. We spoke in detail about some of the challenges she has faced in her life and career, including times of extremely high-pressure when she was going through a tough divorce, working full time while raising three kids, struggling with the death of her estranged mother, and finding out that one of her children had Burkitt lymphoma (thankfully he's okay). When I told her I was wondering whether joy had played a part in helping her be resilient through these challenges, this was her enthusiastic response:

I have really, really strong feelings about joy. I recall a conversation I had many years ago when I was trying to build a foundation with a would-be business partner. I remember saying I thought my purpose in life was to have fun. This was met with a lot of judgment. I heard comments about how life is supposed to be about service and sacrifice. I kept thinking, *No, no, I'm on this planet to have a great time.* Not that everything has to be a great time, but I'm here in this world to be happy, have fun, and experience all of life. That's my value, my stake in the ground.

I do believe that life is about service, but I don't think we need to sacrifice to be of service. And on a deeper level, a person is in their innermost sense of integrity when they're having fun and doing what they love, so when we're doing what we love, we can be of better service to other people. Maybe it's helping people and maybe it's not. For me, it's just knowing there's a girl out there somewhere who sees me doing it and now believes she can too.

Spoelstra emphasizes the need for a balance between self-sacrifice and prioritizing our well-being. My view is similar. Before joining the corporate world, I was newly divorced, had a four-year-old daughter, and was running my own business. And what did I do? I added to my plate by becoming the assistant director for the Miami HEAT Dancers. At the time, I was a single mom with a young child, running my own business while being the assistant director to one of the most popular dance teams in the NBA. I could've crumbled under the pressure, and there were times I felt I might, but I instead focused on what brought me joy: my daughter and dance.

I took Alexandrea everywhere with me, even to rehearsals and games, and she participated in all my cheer and dance alumni events for both the NBA and the NFL.

She then went on to dance competitively, even landing a high school fine arts scholarship, and now she's pursuing a fashion business degree. She continues to take dance classes; in fact, I received a text from her that she's taking ballet.

Now when we go to Miami HEAT games, we run into friends from the office staff and security who have worked for the group for years, and they cannot believe how my baby has turned into a young adult. She basically grew up with them, and the arena is her home away from home.

You might be saying, "You were a single mom with a young child doing all of this? How stressful!" But it really was a total stress release. I needed to do this as a de-stressor so that I could find joy and keep going. And guess what? My hobby, my passion that I was able to perform at the highest level and was my number one stress relief, not only brought

me enjoyment but gave my daughter the gift of a high school education. It also brought so many relationships into our lives. If I can do that as a newly divorced mom with a four-year-old, then so can you.

Taking care of myself through embracing my joy was one of the greatest gifts I gave my daughter because my actions showed her how to take care of herself. For you, it may not be your children, but other people are watching you. You're setting an example whether you realize it or not. Some of us grew up in an environment that never really valued joy and happiness. That was the case with my mother. She was always focused solely on making other people happy, so it was never a part of her process to think about what made her happy; it's been a foreign concept to her throughout her life. We are breaking that cycle.

For those of you who are still rolling your eyes, thinking, *Okay great. Let's go dance and all my problems will be solved*, I just want to say that it's okay. Just stop and go find what brings you joy. Joy will help you.

THE IMPACT OF JOY

There are so many things vying for our attention at home, at work, and in society that it's getting harder and harder to manage our lives. Finding joy can feel frivolous in comparison, and a lot of people think it's just fluff, particularly in the workplace. Many say they simply don't have time for joy. But research shows that employees who experience joy at work tend to demonstrate elevated levels of creativeness and problem-solving capabilities.[2] Leaders who do give themselves time for joy are able to go slow to go fast. With countless matters competing for our time and attention, it's vital to prioritize adding joy to our lives. It's a simple, actionable, and preventative safeguard against stress that could lead to burnout.

Joy impacts us both individually and organizationally. Individually, especially these days, we're more isolated and separated from others due to factors such as AI communication and remote working. And even when we are at work and surrounded by others, we can still feel separated from our team members, which makes us feel lonely. If you take a moment—even three seconds—to get to a place where you can reenergize yourself and feel that sense of joy, you can better meet challenges, both those you give to yourself because you want to grow and those that happen unexpectedly. Joy gives you a place you can go, a place you always have within you and can take anywhere. You just have to reach inside and grab those moments.

According to Mental Health America, "Good feelings can boost your ability to bounce back from stress, solve problems, think flexibly, and even fight disease," and creating joy and satisfaction is a proven tool for resiliency.[3] So on an individual level, discovering proactive activities that increase our confidence and sense of control, those that give us a feeling of being "in the zone" and bring us a sense of accomplishment, allows us to bask in the joy of the doing.

Organizationally, joy helps us show up as the best leaders for our teams. For example, if I'm in a big meeting and feeling stressed or anxious, I visualize myself in a bubble, a protective safe space I can create wherever I am. I take three deep breaths (no one even notices), then visualize myself hitting a golf ball or being outside smelling my roses, two big joys of mine. As long as I'm in that space, I relax a bit and can focus on what I need to do for my clients. For you, it could be something as simple as stepping outside your office and feeling the sun. These are very simple joys, but they're joys we rarely give ourselves time for. Yet when we do, we often find ourselves saying, "Oh my goodness, I should've done this a long time ago!" We come out on the other side refreshed and able to take the next step within our organization and get to the next level.

I remember leading an employee assistance program team through a guided breathing exercise before a virtual meeting. Every team member resided in different locations across the nation. Even though the team understood the importance of well-being and advocated for it throughout the organization and for their clients, they didn't realize just how much they needed to take care of themselves. I explained the benefits of *their* mental well-being, and everyone engaged in the exercise of taking three deep breaths, including the executive team leader. One participant remarked how surprised he was that he felt reenergized after the exercise and was empowered to work on his projects with renewed energy for the rest of the day.

There is power in slowing down and taking care of yourself before speeding back up to the finish line. NASCAR drivers do it all the time during a race. Refueling and getting touch-ups along the way is essential.

Discovering joy as an individual directly influences discovering joy in the workplace. With intentional intervention and employee engagement, joy can be achieved in the workplace, serving as a solution to stress and burnout, and creating resilient corporate cultures.[4] Since laughter is the sound of joy, bringing laughter into our organizations has a significant impact on us both physically and psychologically. Employees perceive leaders who have a sense of humor as significantly more inspiring and admirable than leaders who don't; their employees are more engaged, and their teams are far more likely to solve a challenge creatively, factors that translate into improved performance.[5] Implementing humor in the workplace can even be lucrative. Ending a sales pitch with a joke, for example, can increase the chances that a customer will pay by up to 18%.[6]

Among these and many other benefits, laughter

- lowers blood pressure, soothes tension, enhances mood, and strengthens the immune system;[7]
- reduces inflammation and prevents arterial plaque build-up by releasing nitric oxide;[8]
- reverses the stress response by decreasing stress hormones and increasing "feel-good" hormones that help combat stress and illness;[9] and
- improves quality of life by providing relief from pain, including pain associated with chronic conditions, autoimmune conditions, and even cancer.[10]

Overall, then, joy

- alleviates symptoms of depression and anxiety,
- is an effective coping strategy for emotional distress,
- improves relationships and enhances social interactions by positively impacting mental well-being,
- provides a temporary escape from a stressful environment, and
- helps professionals manage stress and prevent burnout, leading to enhanced satisfaction at work.

Indeed, joy and humor are like magic. As two professors at Stanford University's Graduate School of Business note, "It's up to all of us—and especially leaders—to bring more of it into our workplaces, thereby boosting our well-being, team performance, and even our organizations' bottom lines. Now more than ever, it's time to take humor seriously."[11]

Ultimately, being able to see the humor in everyday life not only enhances our individual well-being but brings teams together. Especially if you're in the healthcare and mental health industries, you work on some serious initiatives. However, as you implement amazing products and services to help people with their holistic health, know that it's okay for you to have fun along the way. It can help lighten the mood as you maneuver through some tough but necessary decisions that must be made and will impact the lives of many.

For me, having fun at work is always a must-have, which is why I start my meetings with a joke. Joy lightens the mood, and laughter unites people. It sets the stage for a safe and inclusive environment. I was teaching a nationwide course on coaching and mentoring to HR professionals who were feeling what we normally feel when walking into something new: trepidation about expectations and how things would go. They were wondering whether they should speak up only when asked or stay quiet and not potentially embarrass themselves. And guess what? When there was a lull, I interjected with a corny joke. I got some giggles, and people began to open up, engage, and share their expertise. It was amazing to see the transformation brought on by a laugh. We all had smiles for the rest of our time together, even though we were embarking on some new territory. I like to think they were laughing with me and not at me. Regardless, a fun time was had while learning.

BARRIERS TO FINDING JOY

The journey of exploring the vital role of joy and resilience in our professional lives brings us to a crucial question: What obstacles do we encounter in integrating joyful activities into our daily routines? As part of our LinkedIn survey, we asked participants this very question. Of the participants surveyed, 50% said it was a lack of time, with workplace demands and stress being significant additional barriers to incorporating self-care.

I've found immense value in dance for my own well-being, but I understand that embracing self-care activities can sometimes be easier said than done. Experts note that the tendency of our societal culture is to avoid creative questions and seek quick fixes instead.[12] Our fast-paced lives frequently prevent us from engaging in reflective discussions before making decisions. Whether it's the hustle of our daily schedules, workplace pressures, fluctuating energy levels, or uncertainty about which activities might enrich our lives, these challenges can often derail our best intentions for self-care. To better understand and address these challenges, it's vital to become more insightful about our experiences. Those insights are invaluable because they help us tailor our approach to better serve ourselves and provide our community with shared understanding and potential strategies to overcome these barriers.

Powerful questions remove barriers. When we take the time to ask the proper questions rather than assuming we have the correct answers, we gain better insight and understanding of our similarities and ignite inclusion among our diverse experiences. Overcoming barriers and moving towards solutions comes only after we obtain and synthesize knowledge, which in turn enhances the culture of our organizations.

We create space for others to contribute by asking questions that encourage deeper thinking beyond a simple yes or no. These often stem from open-ended, nonjudgmental queries that lay a foundation of trust. For executive coaches like me, it's essential to master the art of asking such questions and then actively listening to responses. Guided by intuition and subconscious feeling, this skill allows us to discern what to ask next; though, it is a practice that develops over time.

In a workplace coaching and mentoring class for HR professionals that I facilitated, participants highlighted the strength they gained by asking powerful questions, particularly as a way to guide their own problem-solving rather than only providing answers for their coaches. In my own corporate experience, asking powerful questions has helped me and others achieve personal and professional goals. Here are some questions I've asked myself, interviewers, and supervisors:

1. What are one or two things that stood out to you in your performance this year?
2. Was there anything that surprised you?
3. What is the one key goal you have for the upcoming year that could transform everything?
4. On a scale of 1 to 10, how confident are you in meeting your goal?
5. What is one thing you could do to make the upcoming year a huge success?

These questions have been instrumental in advancing both my personal and professional growth by fostering reflective thinking and strategic planning.

A SIMPLE PATH TO JOY

Many of us start our days by scrolling through our cell phones, whether to check social media, read emails, or distract ourselves with photos, videos, and games. I was doing that once when I found an insightful article about work–life balance in Inc. magazine that reminded me that our seemingly minor choices actually matter a great deal. As I read, I began to formulate the content and carve out some of the key points to creating a simple path to joy and success: The simplicity of building a happy life is based on the little things we do that are within our span of control. We can control how we spend our free time, and it's easy to change our leisure activities.

Research shows that hobbies remove stress, increase resilience, heighten creativity, and help us improve our work performance.[13] The same studies also show that social hobbies make people a great deal happier than solo ones. Now here's the even more interesting part: Out of 27 leisure activities, online activities bring people the least joy. At the top of that list are texting, email, social media, and browsing the internet—all the things most of us wake up to each morning! The only activities people liked less than being online were things like commuting, being sick in bed, and dealing with administration or finances. Wow, what a comparison!

Leisure activities that brought people the most happiness include these joyful ones:

1. Attending performances
2. Going to museums and libraries
3. Exercising and playing sports
4. Gardening

5. Performing music

6. Hanging out with friends

7. Being out in nature

Looking over this list, I see all the activities I enjoy and a variety of activities that my husband and kids also enjoy. Joy is attainable, and scoping out the time for self-care is important.

One of my favorite quotes is about understanding everything better by looking deep into nature. I think of it often when I'm spending time outdoors. A few years ago, I planted a mango tree. My neighbors across from me and beside me have enormous, fully grown, 25-year-old trees that produce the sweetest mangoes, and they share them with me every mango season. I love mangoes, look forward to mango season, and appreciate my neighbors' generosity. So does my family because I tend to share the wealth. I decided I wanted to have mangoes grown in my backyard, so I planted my own. One day, unexpectedly, I saw the buds of mangoes on my tree. Oh the excitement!

The corner near the mango tree is my magical place. It's my place to think, a place where I allow my mind to be imaginative. It's where I feel most in charge of setting boundaries for myself so I can create space—space to think, write, strategize, heal, and love. I think about living life differently, with less stress and more love. Love is the answer to everything, after all. By the corner of the mango tree, I see how life mimics nature. Every time I look at the mango tree, I see something new. Some fruit is hidden behind leaves, some peek out with the brush of the wind, and some are waiting for me to discover them tomorrow. What a delight!

It's the simple things that bring joy into our lives. Since the pandemic, I've noticed that I rely on seven small joys to brighten each day:[14]

1. Enjoying a morning beverage
2. Getting outside
3. Talking to friends
4. Taking a nap
5. Reading a book / Listening to an audiobook
6. Laughing
7. Hanging out, doing nothing

From starting my day with a brisk morning walk while listening to a podcast or audiobook to slowly drinking a hot cup of chai, taking time to connect with my family and friends, or just spending time alone to do nothing but think, I make time for joy and what it brings. And this is where magic happens. Peace of mind not only makes you a healthier you with better connections to your loved ones, but also leads to innovative ideas and strategies.

Change is hard, especially when it comes to changing the big things in life, such as a career, a spouse, and where we live. But changing what we do during our time away from work is easy, and it could bring us more immediate joy. That's why as often as possible I get offline and enjoy time with my family and friends.

WHERE IS YOUR JOY?

Preparation is essential for navigating the unexpected changes in life, whether they're perceived as positive or negative. Often, we realize the full impact of these opportunities only in hindsight when reflecting on how they shaped us. It's important to step back and assess yourself, not just to understand who you were in the past but to understand who you are now. I've created a reflective exercise in the Reader Resources section at the back of this book, and I encourage you to investigate your current state of joy. Here are some questions to help you start this self-reflection:

➤ How joyful are you?

➤ What barriers are keeping you from finding joy?

➤ How might a lack of joy be impacting your life?

➤ When was the last time you stopped and smelled the roses?

➤ What activities bring you the most joy? Make you feel relaxed? Give you inner peace? Make you excited about repeating? Make you feel energized?

➤ How do these activities help you stay resilient at work?

➤ How much time do you spend doing joyful activities?

➤ Who else is involved in these activities with you? How does sharing the activity with others heighten the feeling of joy?

➤ Do you teach others this activity? If so, how does it feel when your learners experience joy through the activity?

KEANE INSIGHTS. **KEANE INSIGHT**: One of the easiest ways to bring more joy into your life is to change how you spend your time away from work. I recommend creating a "Joy Menu," which is a list of simple things that bring you joy and recharge your energy. It's often the little things that help us find joy and build resilience, preparing us to handle whatever comes our way.

KEANE
INSIGHTS.

Create Your Joy Menu™

Adding more joy to your life can reduce stress. Create your personalized Joy Menu selecting 5-10 personal favorite activities brings you joy.

Organize these activities into categories (e.g., daily or weekly) for easy integration into your routine. Schedule time to engage with them and start gradually, staying flexible and updating your menu as needed. Celebrate the positive impact on your mood and resilience as you embrace these joyful moments.

1. Selected Activities:

1.

2.

3.

4.

5.

6.

7.

8.

9.

10.

When you take time to step away from the chaos and noise of everyone and everything around you, you can listen to your heart's desires. You can think clearly without interruption. Where does this happen for you? Some of my friends who are speakers say it's while they're at the airport or on a plane. For me, it's in the quiet moments in the morning before everyone is awake and in the nights after everyone has gone to sleep. It's in the drives to and from work, while shopping or going somewhere, and when I take a 20-minute walk around my neighborhood. Even now as I write, I'm in my bubble, writing without interruption.

Each of us needs to carve out some time to be alone, think, process, and strategize. Usually that's done when we're doing something for ourselves, something we enjoy doing. What do you like to do? When you get immersed in it, you have a sense of freedom. You could do it for hours and be totally at peace. This is the state of mind where creativity comes from.

Creativity expands when freed from the grips of stress. By identifying and managing stress through finding those peaceful moments where we can truly unwind, we open the door to creativity and innovation. Invite these moments into your life and watch how they transform your ability to think and create.

Presentations

Inspiring presentations that energize leaders through personal stories and actionable strategies to foster joy, resilience, and effective leadership within teams and organizations.

CHAPTER 2

FINDING JOY AMID STRESS

Why was the computer stressed after work?
Because it had a hard drive!

~Anonymous

What is the number one stressor for you at work? As you think about that stressor, notice how you feel. What thoughts pop up in your mind? How is your body reacting? Do you recognize any of these signs of burnout at home?

- Noticing bags under your eyes from sleeping too much or too little
- Seeing numbers fluctuate on the scale due to overindulging or not eating enough
- Avoiding feelings by overscheduling yourself
- Binge-watching shows and movies and obsessively watching the same ones
- Isolating yourself from loved ones and avoiding familiar activities

- Feeling dizzy or noticing other physical manifestations, such as headaches, muscle pain, or gastrointestinal issues
- Experiencing brain fog and forgetting things or getting confused easily
- Second-guessing yourself and wondering whether you're overreacting
- Feeling irritated all the time, even by little things[15]

How about these signs of burnout at work?

- Feeling angry and cynical towards work and quickly getting irritated with your coworkers, even over trivial matters
- Experiencing anxiety about work that won't go away and negatively impacts your life outside of work
- Detaching from your coworkers and work responsibilities
- Being unable to focus on your work tasks
- Noticing a decline in your productivity and quality of work
- Hating your job and workplace
- Feeling unmotivated to start tasks and losing the will to complete them
- Believing your efforts at work don't matter
- Feeling a sense of loss of control and influence over your work[16]

Perhaps not surprisingly, persistent and pervasive stress at work is the leading cause of burnout. According to the World Health Organization, "Burnout is a syndrome conceptualized as resulting from chronic workplace stress that has not been successfully managed."[17] And in one of their largest studies on the topic, Gallup found that the main culprit is our leaders, particularly "unfair treatment at work . . . an unmanageable workload, unclear communication from managers, lack of manager support, and unreasonable time pressure."[18] Leaders must address these factors to reduce their staff's burnout, especially if they want their organizations to thrive.

With stress levels increasing all over the world and our managers causing us burnout, it's time to look at how we can add positivity. As Alexandrea wisely said during the COVID-19 pandemic, "The world needed to slow down." Stress is something we collectively have to be aware of and prepared for, and we can do that only when we take the time to slow down and pay attention to how stress is impacting our lives. Let's start by defining stress.

WHAT STRESS REALLY IS

A widely used definition of stress is that "the demands of a situation threaten to exceed the resources of the individual."[19] One thing I always find interesting when looking at these more academic definitions of stress is that the perception of the individual is always listed as a key contributing factor. I bristle at that because we often have a fight-or-flight response when we perceive danger, and the danger is not always a physical one–such as facing a wild animal that may want to attack us. It can also be something like the need to get a project done before an important deadline; our perception of the importance of that deadline will affect our stress level about completing the project. Unfortunately, the body doesn't know the difference between a wild animal and a project deadline, so the amygdala in the brain triggers that fight-or-flight response whether we like it or not.

"Are you telling me this is all in my head, Nicole?" No, I'm not saying stress is all in anyone's head. Feelings of stress are usually triggered by some outside event. There are many common events in today's workplaces and throughout society that reliably provoke feelings of stress. I've been there. For now, as we move on, the main thing I want you to keep in mind is that stress is essentially an internal response—a feeling, if you will—that occurs in response to an external challenging situation. Let's break this down.

External stress often stems from real, tangible situations, and while perception plays a role, the triggers are often very real. It's a feeling that arises in reaction to challenging circumstances, such as discovering that a loved one has been diagnosed with cancer.

One of my previous external stressors was that I found myself part of the "sandwich generation," balancing the care of parents over the age of 65 with the care of a child younger than 18 and two young-adult children in college, making up our blended family. I vividly remember the mixed emotions I felt while parenting and caring for my father, who had been diagnosed with pancreatic cancer. Although it required a significant amount of time and energy, it also brought our family closer together. Supporting my parents during this time allowed me to honor them by caring for my father and alleviating some of the burden from my mother. They have always done so much for others, and this was my chance to care for and love them as they have always cared for and loved me and many others throughout my life.

But stress doesn't always come from "out there." Stress comes from how we *react* to an external situation, which comes from inside. I spoke with Josh Landay, who refocused his career from performing internationally in *The Lion King* to being the executive director of the nonprofit organization Gifted Savings after his wife was diagnosed with cancer. He agrees that "If you think about tension in general, and if a situation is already tense, if you become even more rigid, it's only going to add to that . . . Whereas if you remain flexible, you take in the situation that's going on and say, 'How best do I respond to the situation?' And don't just respond with initial instinct or impulse, but rather try to take it in and be thoughtful about it, and then respond."

As leaders, we frequently impose pressure on ourselves to be perfect. Transitioning from a fixed mindset where perfection is the goal to a growth mindset where mistakes are seen as opportunities is crucial. This shift helps us understand how mistakes can lead to innovation. During one of Keane Insights' live resilience sessions, for instance, a CEO of a nonprofit organization shared her new perspective on mistakes. She now views them as opportunities, which has significantly reduced her stress about making errors.

A common misconception is that doing everything flawlessly will lead to success. However, it's often *through* our imperfections or perceived failures that we experience breakthroughs that propel us to higher levels and create unforeseen opportunities. Embracing our imperfections can elevate us to new heights.

You might be saying, "I know what stress feels like, but why can't I control it?" Because stress is an internal response to external pressure, and while we can manage our responses to some extent, the stress itself isn't something we feel we can completely control. Stress can also manifest in various ways that affect both our mental and our physical health. Stress is the body's way of responding to any kind of demand or threat. When we sense danger—whether real or imagined—the body's defenses kick into high gear in that rapid, automatic response of fight or flight, otherwise known as the stress response. And what happens then? During an interview I had with him, accomplished comedian, actor, and author Finesse Mitchell summed it up: "Nobody likes being around a stressed and burned-out person. You're short with your answers, you're snappy at people, and people are always trying to walk on eggshells. But that's the definition of being stressed and burned out. So realize that first, and try to get ahold of it. Try to get that under control. Because you can't do anything good, especially if you need other people's help."

Understanding the nature of stress and how it affects us is the first step in managing it. This shift in mindset also enhances self-awareness, a crucial component of resilience both personally and professionally. Recognizing when we need to reconnect with ourselves is vital for maintaining resilience and fostering individual and organizational growth.

TYPES OF STRESS

We're affected by all types of stress, but most fall into two categories: acute and chronic. Acute stress is when we perceive immediate danger. It's typically short-lived and subsides once the perceived threat or stressful event has passed. Having a fight with a loved one or being in a car accident are two examples. Approximately 5%–20% of individuals develop acute stress disorder following a traumatic or highly stressful event. We can experience acute stress temporarily without developing a medical condition, but persistent symptoms can result in a diagnosis of acute stress disorder.[20]

Chronic stress, on the other hand, is the kind of stress that lasts for a long time without a break. It's often caused by things like persistent unmanageable workloads at our jobs, ongoing conflicts or relationship issues, or being in a toxic work environment day after day. Have you ever felt that?

The defining feature of chronic stress is that unlike the stress that builds before a big event then subsides when it's over, chronic stress doesn't go away. It's there all the time, and it can cause some serious problems, including high blood pressure, heart disease, anxiety, depression, and a weakened immune system. Have you ever experienced that?

Chronic stress is extremely common. In response to the effects of COVID-19 on people's mental health, the American Psychological Association conducted a survey called "Stress in America 2023." The study showed that on a scale of 1 to 10, nearly one-quarter of adults surveyed rated their average stress between 8 and 10. When asked about what was stressing them out the most, the most common responses were money and the economy, health problems, family responsibilities, housing costs, and personal safety.[21] This part is significant because what do you notice about those top responses? They don't go away.

You might be wondering what all this has to do with resilience. When we talk about resilience, we're really discussing the ability to stay strong in the face of stress. Our perceptions of stress are crucial because our body's fight or flight response activates when we feel *any* level of stress. By choosing how we perceive a given stressor, we can better manage our reactions to it. This shift in perception and response enhances our resilience, allowing us to handle stress more effectively and maintain our well-being.

The persistent nature of stressors highlights the critical role of resilience in maintaining mental and physical health. Resilience can act as a shield against the adverse effects of chronic stress. Studies show that individuals with a higher degree of resilience experience fewer stress-related health issues and report healthier overall well-being than those with lower levels,[22] and resilience training programs in workplaces can lead to reduced employee burnout and increased job satisfaction.[23] These findings underscore the critical role of resilience in managing ongoing stressors effectively.

THE IMPACT OF STRESS IN THE WORKPLACE

The way we handle stress significantly impacts our overall health and well-being. While having a strong work ethic and a commitment to a mission are admirable qualities, these traits can become detrimental when combined with a toxic environment. If our stress is left unchecked in these conditions, it can lead to serious consequences.

Chronic stress often leads to mental health issues. According to the US Department of Labor, "Stress can be harmful to our health and increase mental health challenges [including] clinical mental illness and substance use disorders as well as other emotions like stress, grief, feeling sad and anxious, where these feelings are temporary and not part of a diagnosable condition. While there are many things in life that induce stress, work can be one of those factors."[24] In the workplace, such stress directly impacts our job performance, our productivity, and our engagement and communication, and outside of work stress also impacts our physical capabilities and daily functioning. Thus, stress is an essential topic in workplace mental health for three main reasons:

1. Chronic stress can mimic a mental health condition.

2. Unhealthy stress can worsen preexisting mental health conditions.

3. Prolonged, high-level stress can lead to burnout.

Workplace stress is more specific than general stress. The CDC defines workplace stress as "the harmful physical and emotional responses that occur when the requirements of a job do not match the capabilities, resources, or needs of the worker."[25] In our experiences at Keane Insights, as well as through collecting much research on the topic, we've learned that many upper managers and C-suite executives tend to deal with workplace stress in unhealthy ways:

1. Overworking and neglecting personal time by immersing themselves in work to the detriment of personal time and rest.

2. Turning to alcohol, prescription drugs, or other substances for temporary relief.

3. Ignoring or denying the root causes of their stress and not facing unresolved issues.

4. Relying on fast food or skipping meals, negatively impacting their health and energy.

5. Neglecting physical activity that's crucial for managing stress and maintaining health.

6. Sacrificing sleep for work, ultimately diminishing their cognitive functions and increasing their stress.

7. Distancing themselves from friends, family, and colleagues, leading to a lack of social support.

8. Engaging in negative self-talk and speaking pessimistically, worsening their symptoms of burnout.

9. Coping through unhealthy mechanisms such as engaging in excessive gaming, online distractions, or other time-wasting activities that don't address stress.

10. Micromanaging every detail, increasing their stress and that of their teams while reducing overall productivity and morale.

Personally, I really had to find out what my stressors were and learn to adapt successfully in the face of overwhelming pressure. When I started practicing family therapy, I spent my time hearing everyone's problems, and at the end of each day I felt completely drained. After hearing all these traumatic stories, it was difficult for me to detach. I realized I was taking a lot of them home with me, and they became my stressors, so much so that it was negatively affecting me. I felt like waves were crushing me. I was jumpy, even at little things, and I developed migraine headaches. Though I couldn't sleep at night, I couldn't stay awake at the dinner table. I finally realized how stressed out I was. In order to ride the waves and not be crushed, I had to adapt and tap into my de-stressors.

You may be experiencing similar issues. If so, Josh Landay offers this advice: "If there isn't a why within the work that I'm doing, then it's only stress. If you can dial up the purpose and dial up the joy within that, that proportionally makes the stress somewhat lower. It doesn't necessarily dial it down, it just dials up that good, which makes those things outweigh the stress."

THE INTERPLAY BETWEEN STRESS AND JOY

Joy can come from engaging in leisurely activities that reduce stress. In fact, engaging in leisure activities has helped many CEOs of Fortune 500 companies as well as S&P 500 companies and comparable organizations not only cope with the stress of their executive jobs but also support their optimal functioning and leadership effectiveness.[26] This further emphasizes the importance of being joyful, yet many still consider joy an unattainable goal. As Liza Rossi pointed out, "People often struggle to find joy because they lack the tools to access it, leaving them feeling stuck. But when they gain access to those tools, it can make all the difference."

I'm sometimes asked, "Does joy have a formula?" Yes, it does. I found it while navigating the stressful landscape of divorce.

When I was a little girl, I used to watch the women in my family cook. I would sit on a stool at the kitchen table, dangling my little feet over the edge, and I would inhale the aromas. My mom and aunts would talk to me while they cooked, telling me about their secret ingredients for all their traditional food, including macaroni and cheese, fried fish, peas and rice, potato salad, coleslaw, and my mom's infamous friendship cake. Each recipe was written on a card, and all the cards lived in a recipe box. One recipe card in this box was probably the most important card of all, a card of advice that has been with me my whole life and is ingrained in my subconscious: the recipe for a happy life. These women weren't just teaching me how to make cake or macaroni and cheese; they were teaching me about life and how to have a joyful one.

As we grow up, we make a recipe for what we think will bring us happiness and joy. I used to think joy meant getting the things I wanted. And before I actually had joy in my life, I thought it was being in the right place at the right time; that it was circumstantial and just happened. Like many people, I added to my recipe for happiness a spouse, a child, and a nice house. I checked all the boxes until I thought I'd made the perfect joyful life, complete with a ring, a house, a child, and a happy family picture on the wall. We even planned to take an international cruise and visit the wonders of the world. Life had given me the winning recipe for what happily ever after looked like, but it had been passed down over time through the women in my family and then through society. I was living life according to my recipe, but it was a recipe for what I *thought* my life should look like.

Then I got a divorce.

He was supposed to be the one. Everything I thought about myself and my whole identity—my main source of joy—was gone. And I'd done everything "right." But one moment in couples counseling, it finally hit me once and for all that it was over. He didn't want to work on our marriage. It was done. And just like that, my happily-ever-after cake crumbled to the floor, along with my recipe for a happy life.

Everything I had defined in my world to bring me joy got ripped out from under me and came crashing down. I was a single mother with a young child, on my own and feeling really lonely, wondering whether I'd ever find love again and have the family I always dreamed of. Since my joy was gone, I lost myself in other things. I absorbed myself in work, and I went through the motions expecting that joy would just come to me.

Then, one ordinary day, I was in my backyard pruning my rose bushes, literally smelling the roses. (As you'll learn throughout this book, being around the beauty of nature brings me a sense of calm and peace.) I looked up to see Alexandrea watching me through the kitchen window. When I went inside a bit later, she said, "Mom, you haven't smiled like that in a long time. I miss that smile." I didn't even realize that gardening was a calming agent for me until she said that. At that moment, it occurred to me that when I was in the garden, I was doing something that brought me joy.

While living in stress and waiting for joy to find me, I realized that it's okay to do things for myself first, and I began to redesign my life. I'm the cook in my own kitchen now. I get to create the recipes. And like me, you get to be the cook in your kitchen and create your own recipe for joy. Joy isn't something you have to wait for. It's something you can pursue, even amid stress.

Oh, and by the way, when I least expected it, a new charming prince did come riding up. Turns out, he was even better for me than the first. And this time, I was ready for him to walk alongside me as we built our happily-ever-after together.

HOW IS STRESS AFFECTING YOU?

I don't know what your stressors are, as they depend on our position and experiences, but we can agree that we all have them. Let's face it: We can all get stressed about changes and challenges that are happening all around us, and sometimes we bring work stress home. Being proactive about implementing more joy into our lives is a means to stress management, and what better way to manage stress than through healthy and joyful activities? The first step to alleviating the effects of stress in your life is to identify your biggest stressors.

When you get home exhausted from a stressful day at work, when you feel completely burned out, what are some of your pet peeves? Think about something that really gets on your nerves when you get home from work. If you work remotely, think about something that gets on your nerves when you switch from work mode to home mode. For instance, if

I came home and found the sink filled with dirty dishes yet again? Oh, that's one of my biggest pet peeves!

In part 2, we'll be exploring in detail how stress is impacting you in specific aspects of your life and work. In preparation, let's start thinking about your general well-being and your most significant stressors.

➤ General questions:

- How stressed are you?

- How do you feel when you're stressed?

- What symptoms of burnout do you recognize in yourself?

- How are you sleeping at night?

- How is your overall health?

- How do you feel about going back to work after a couple of days off?

- Are you avoiding the source(s) of your stress?

➤ What are your five biggest stressors or pet peeves?

1. _____

2. _____

3. _____

4. _____

5. _____

➤ How do you usually cope with these stressors?

- Alcohol, drugs, and/or smoking

- Exercising
- Eating junk food
- Lashing out
- Breathing and/or mindfulness practices
- Other: _____

➤ How do you think these stressors might be impacting you?

1. _____

2. _____

3. _____

4. _____

5. _____

A few years ago, I made a list of 100 ways to reduce stress, each of which has added health and emotional well-being to my life by helping me prioritize joy through self-care. You'll find the full list at the end of this chapter, as well as in the Reader Resources section at the back of the book. I encourage you to review the list and find what works for you. Here are the five I find particularly helpful:

1. Visualizing a relaxing scene
2. Saying no when needed
3. Laughing often
4. Finding a quiet spot to relax
5. Meditating

With stress levels increasing all over the world, we're going through a crisis. In fact, it's gotten so bad that The White House has declared mental health as a national crisis, which the CDC reports 90% of adults are experiencing. This further highlights the gravity of the situation. It's time to look at how we can add positivity to our lives even in this difficult time. By identifying our stressors and finding effective ways to cope with them, such as enjoying the simple things in life, we begin to discover the pathway to self-care, which is the bridge from stress to resilience.

KEANE INSIGHT: A key strategy for ensuring success is managing stress effectively. Stress is a part of life, but proactivity in how you handle it can make all the difference. I suggest taking a few minutes at the end of each day to reflect on what triggered your stress, how you responded, and what you learned. It's also helpful to engage in a simple 5-minute self-care activity—small actions that keep you feeling joyful and ready to take on new challenges.

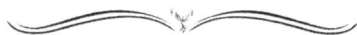

When we're going through so much, filled with worry and fear instead of just resiliently pushing through with such a heavy load, sometimes we need to adapt by lightening the load so that we can thrive forward. But how do we do that when we're impacted by loss, stress, and constant change? By "putting down the glass" and taking our 15-minute breaks throughout the day, our full lunch away from the computer, and our PTO without checking into work. We do this to take care of ourselves so that we can reenergize and become more productive. When we truly unplug, we allow ourselves to be energized in a way that when we come back, we are a force to add even greater value, both personally and professionally.

Another key theme related to stress is change, which is what we're really talking about when we're discussing stress. And change is a funny thing. Even when we know it's probably for the best, whether for our personal lives or for the workplace, change can be HARD. But that's what resilience is for. It allows us to keep it together through a time of change and stress. When we get to the point where we've reaped the benefits of the change—or at least survived it without any lasting harm—then we grow.

Content Licensing

Equip leaders and teams with practical tools to manage mental health, sustain joy, and build resilience under pressure. Access actionable insights to address stigma, strengthen a supportive culture, and implement effective strategies that promote employee well-being.

100 Ways to Reduce Stress™

1. Take 10 deep breaths	26. Exercise	51. Cry if necessary	76. Give a genuine compliment
2. Visualize a relaxing scene	27. Plan ahead	52. Be flexible	77. Express gratitude
3. Learn to say no	28. Talk with a friend	53. Don't procrastinate	78. Call a good friend
4. Stay clutter-free	29. Dance	54. Wear earplugs when it's noisy	79. Wear comfortable clothes
5. Read good books	30. Laugh at yourself	55. Enjoy aromatherapy	80. Take off your shoes
6. Stretch	31. Count your blessings	56. Spend time with loved ones	81. Forgive and forget
7. Write in a journal	32. Be silly	57. Create artwork	82. Delegate work
8. Try yoga	33. Set realistic goals	58. Do one task at a time	83. Love others
9. Laugh often	34. Sing	59. Meditate	84. Have a plant
10. Watch clouds go by	35. Think positively	60. Avoid distractions	85. Daydream
11. Look at a magazine	36. Squeeze a stress ball	61. Budget time and money	86. Help someone else
12. Believe in yourself	37. Eat right	62. Share jokes	87. Bake a special treat
13. Prioritize tasks	38. Take a nap	63. Play games with family	88. Savor meals
14. Get fresh air	39. Walk away	64. Look at the big picture	89. Look at old photos
15. Hug someone	40. Vary your routine	65. Get up earlier	90. Watch a comedy
16. Get plenty of sleep	41. Get a massage	66. Set limits	91. Don't overcommit yourself
17. Watch a movie	42. Ask for help	67. Express your feelings	92. Learn something new
18. Seek out positive people	43. Find a quiet spot to relax	68. Treat yourself to a gift	93. Take a deep breath
19. Make to-do lists	44. Take regular breaks	69. Simplify your life	94. Treat yourself to frozen yogurt
20. Take a brisk walk	45. Listen to soothing music	70. Reflect on your joys	95. Join an online group
21. Stargaze	46. See problems as challenges	71. Plant a tree	96. Rub your neck and shoulders
22. Sip a cup of herbal tea	47. Smile often	72. Take a full lunch break	97. Provide encouragement to others
23. Put your feet up	48. Be faithful	73. Don't dwell on the past	98. Recognize beauty around you
24. Enjoy a hobby	49. Avoid caffeine and tobacco	74. Play with a pet	99. Take it one day at a time
25. Confront your feelings	50. Eat a good breakfast	75. Soak in the tub	100. Make someone smile

CHAPTER 3

BUILDING RESILIENCE

*Yesterday I saw the most famous rubber band in the world.
It was the center of a-tension.*

~Anonymous

We've all heard, especially in recent years, that there are certain things we need to do to grow our resilience, such as get enough sleep, drink enough water throughout the day, eat healthily, engage in yoga, meditate, and take deep breaths. These self-care practices are important for toughing things out, but I take a different view and am going to share with you what no one else is telling you. There are two ways to be resilient: through toughness and through flexibility. Our approach at Keane Insights is about flexibility. It's the formula for springing back into shape after a change or challenge.

WHAT RESILIENCE IS ALL ABOUT

Resilience means different things to different people. During our interview, I asked Nikki Spoelstra what resilience means to her:

Being resilient has a lot to do with being scared sometimes and not knowing what the future will hold for
you. By trusting your deepest sense of inner knowing, your North Star of sorts, you protect yourself,
put yourself in the best possible position given your
set of circumstances, to move forward in the world in
a way that you feel grounded, fulfilled, and peaceful
and miss potential chaos. Being resilient is about
focusing on what I really want, which is peace in my
heart. Happiness comes and goes. Love comes and
goes. I want to feel peaceful. So when I think about
resilience, I think about coming back and being able
to find a place of peace within yourself. Even in the
hardest and darkest of times, if you can come back
to a place of peace, that to me is resilience.

Spoelstra touches on what resilience is all about: growth. The
whole reason we want to be resilient is that deep down, we all
know change is coming. We all know we're going to face tough
situations that stress us out. And when they come, we want to
be the ones who end up being better, wiser, and more capable
human beings who are ready to face the next challenge.

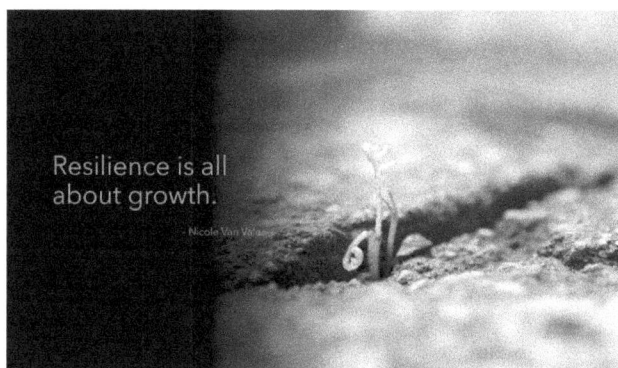

Resilience is all about growth.
- Nicole Van Va'an

Now, I have to admit that I'm an undercover nerd. I read a peer review study on driving performance excellence that noted in working conditions, positive stress actually encourages employees to perform at a higher level. And guess what? Even though I was flooded with nerves, I remembered the choreography during all my performances because it was ingrained in my body from all the rehearsals. Resilience takes practice.

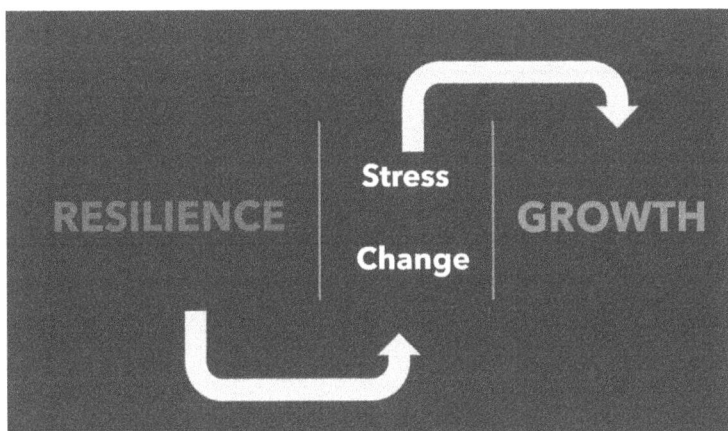

Right now you might be saying, "Nicole, that's all well and good. I appreciate the positive spin. But what about when things don't work out for the better? What about when there's lasting harm from change?" Ahhhh. What do you think? Is there space for resilience when things don't work out? For instance, what if you lose your job, but instead of finding another one right away, an even better one, you just don't, so you lose your house, your car, and your marriage? What about when someone has a car accident and loses a leg or is faced with the significant loss of a loved one? Is that something they should just perk up and think positively about because, if they're resilient, better things are coming their way? Of course not.

Things don't always work out for the better, but that isn't exactly something you want to say to someone in the throes of a traumatic situation. However, there is a phenomenon known as post-traumatic growth, or PTG. The phenomenon refers to "the positive psychological change that some individuals experience after a life crisis or traumatic event."[27] It occurs alongside negative psychological consequences to stress and trauma. People who experience PTG still go through all the bad stuff of stress and trauma, but they also experience personal growth. PTG may feature positive changes in self-perception, relationships, self-awareness, self-confidence, and discovery of new possibilities.

PTG is a whole subject of its own that we're not going to unpack here. But the point is, in the face of stress and change, even during life-changing events, there is always room for growth. And the best way to achieve growth is by being resilient in the face of stress and change. That's our focus: how to ensure we have in place the building blocks required to be resilient and grow through whatever life throws our way. By strengthening our resilience muscles, we can use resilience as our competitive advantage. We can differentiate ourselves and our organizations so that we, and they, can thrive during periods of change.

COMMON CONNECTIONS

Interestingly, in embracing our differences we often discover that we have much in common. I've learned this primarily through building relationships.

One of my favorite things to do as a speaker when attending conferences is to connect with other keynote speakers and panelists. At a National Speakers Association preconference session, I had the pleasure of hearing from Cynt Marshall, CEO of the Dallas Mavericks. She shared her powerful story of witnessing domestic violence as a child, enduring four miscarriages, losing a daughter, and ultimately adopting four children. Inspired by her resilience, I asked her how she managed to think differently and move forward. She answered that her resilience stemmed from one word: *faith*. Her words resonated deeply with me, affirming my passion for resilience and helping those in need. Marshall's story confirmed that I am on the right path, speaking about resilience during these challenging times. Her encouragement to keep going was a profound reminder that faith leads the way to resilience.

I had a similar experience at the 2024 Diversity Alliance for Science Conference. While sitting in the audience, I listened to keynote speaker Hank Azaria, a six-time Emmy Award winner, Screen Actors Guild Award winner, and Tony Award nominee who is most recognized for voicing hundreds of characters on *The Simpsons*. I was moved by his vulnerability in sharing his journey of self-discovery amid one of the most challenging times of his career. When asked how he was able to be resilient through this journey, he described it in one word: *willingness*. He went on to explain that The Human Solidarity Project provided him with a safe environment where he could make connections and have the space and time to learn and discover more about himself and the perspectives of others. During this journey, he not only adjusted his way of thinking but joined forces to increase awareness while having genuine human connection. I must share that I met Azaria the night before his keynote, and the vulnerability and connection he exuded on stage was the same energy he had when I connected with him during our conversation.

Connections like these have given me the opportunity to explore the various facets of resilience through interviewing some noble figures from a variety of industries. Given their roles and achievements, I knew their personal stories could offer valuable perspectives on how joy has helped them be resilient. I was inspired by the strategies and mindsets that have helped them overcome challenges and achieve success. I was also struck by how, although they each defined resilience a bit differently, they all had common connections.

Each interview concluded with me asking one significant question: If you could describe resilience in one word, what would it be?

➤ Adrienne Nicole, Emmy nominated and award-winning producer and founder of Adrienne Nicole Productions, shared the word *bounce*: "Resilience is a bounce-back, so it's either coming back to where you were or going further."

➤ Aria Johnson, a keynote speaker and TV personality, chose the word *love*: "You can fall down, get kicked on the ground, and get back up out of anger, or you can fall down, get kicked on the ground, and get back up out of love because you respect yourself enough to do it. Love is always a higher vibration than anger."

➤ Bruce Turkel, a corporate branding expert, used the word *belief*: "If you believe in what you're doing or believe in what your goal or intention is . . . you'll be resilient. You'll know what you want."

➤ Dr. Taft Parsons III, the chief psychiatric officer for the Fortune 6 company CVS Health, referenced the word *realistic*: "People feel like they have to do everything. Well, it's not realistic. I think that having an orientation to being realistic about what you can and can't do, what anybody can and can't do, kind of helps level what you should be doing in a lot of decision-making processes. So I think a lot of resilience comes from being realistic about [our] capabilities."

➤ Elizabeth Davis, the vice president of National Broker Distribution and Strategy for Medicare Advantage at Cigna, mentioned the word *flexibility*: "I'm bobbing and weaving, and I'm dealing with this, and I'm dealing with that."

➤ Finesse Mitchell identified the word *consistency*: "Consistency is being determined to keep showing up. You gotta keep showing up . . . when you're being resilient, people always see you."

➤ Jeff Hoffman, award-winning global entrepreneur and producer, worldwide motivational speaker, and bestselling author, selected the word *determination*: "I am not going to let whatever is going on in the world around me get me down. I am determined to rise above, I am determined to win, and I am determined not to let the negative energy drown me."

➤ John Register, a Paralympic silver medalist, US Army Combat Veteran, and Certified Professional Keynote Speaker, noted the word *relentlessness*: "In resilience we need to pursue a better tomorrow as a mindset. The other word is *silence*. Embedded in the word resilience is the word silence. We need to find a white spot to collect our thoughts."

➢ Josh Landay, Executive Director of Gifted Savings, chose the word *adaptability:* "People are different everywhere. In every role I've had, people are different. You've got to learn from the people around you. It's not about being fickle; it's learning how to learn and grow based on new situations and new people."

➢ Karélix Alicea, founder and president of Lotus Behavioral Interventions, cofounder of the Miami Association for Behavior Analysis, and the executive director of The Lotus Children, chose the word *power:* "I think we live in power. We breathe in power. We think in power. We have to share that power. We have to connect our power with others. I think resilience is all about power and being able to tap into our internal power, and again, being able to extend it outward . . . I believe we are very, very powerful beings with limitless capacity."

➢ Kelvin McLaurin, Partner at MJK Solutions and Former SVP of Global Business Services at McDonald's Corporation and CVS Health, selected the word *recovery:* "It's the ability to recover from adversity."

➢ Liza Rossi thought of the word *freedom:* "If you can, tap into that inner joy. I think that propels resilience or your journey to being resilient, at least. Tapping into your own joy brings you to a state of freedom."

➢ Mercedes Martin, founder and CEO of Mercedes Martin & Co., said resilience is *regenerative:* "Regenerative means I can stop. I can reenergize. I can get myself back together. I'm thinking about it as where the world is right now. We don't have a chance to sustain; we have to build the resilience to regenerate."

➤ Nadia Turner, a dedicated clinical mental health counselor and professional vocalist, picked the word *fighting*: "I'm not a person who puts stuff out there other than what I want you to see, so no one would ever know that I have to fight for joy. And I have to push through the pain, but what I do behind closed doors is giving myself grace to know that I'm constantly evolving, and I'm evolving for the better."

➤ Pedrya Seymour, an Olympic athlete, selected the word *courage*: "It takes courage to pick yourself up time and time again. For me as an athlete, it takes courage to have a short-term memory; for instance, at the last meet you may have come in last place or had a bad race, but on Monday at practice you have to forget about that race. And it takes courage to do that. It takes courage to keep picking yourself back up."

➤ Robyn Hatcher, CPS and consultant, author and former actor, and former writer for *All My Children* and *One Life to Live*, decided on the word *elasticity*: "It's changeability, like being a boomerang or a trampoline; [it's about being] adaptive."

➤ Sara Derek, founder and CEO of Experience Camps, came up with the word *growth*: "It's all the elements that go into being able to grow in a positive way."

➤ Serin Oh, a singer and songwriter, chose the word *peace*: "Resilience to me is to be peaceful, to have peace . . . and surrendering to the process; peace in the mistake that you've made. True resilience is having peace."

When I asked my family members this question, I discovered they have similar views. My father shared that to him resilience means *adaptability*, noting it's "the ability to adapt to situations whether static or dynamic." My mother, as did Oh, described resilience as *peace* because to her being resilient means being content with where you want to be, which is a peaceful feeling. To my husband, resilience means *fortitude* because it's about strength.

Bounce, love, belief, realistic, flexibility, consistency, determination, relentlessness, adaptability, power, recovery, freedom, regenerative, fighting, courage, elasticity, growth, peace, and fortitude—words and feelings we can all relate to. The amazing thing is that these simple yet profound words represent what we all need to be resilient and to maintain our resiliency, both in our personal lives and across our industries.

My aim in asking all these incredible people this question was to gain expert insights into their career paths, key challenges they've faced, and how they've overcome them, but in turn, doing so helped *me* remain resilient. Asking this one powerful question opened the door to some enlightening conversations and helped me understand how others think. It could do the same for you. Applying their approaches to developing and maintaining resilience, especially during high-pressure situations, might benefit you across the various domains of your personal life and career.

RESILIENCE IN THE WORKPLACE

Research on resilience and its correlation with performance at work found that resilient employees are better able to adapt to organizational changes and less likely to feel burnout, allowing them to improve their mental health and maintain high performance levels.[28] However, only 30% of employees feel their workplace provides the support they need for setting goals for their well-being at work.[29] When we asked participants of our LinkedIn survey how their employers could better support the participants' well-being, 50% said flexible working hours. This further emphasizes the need for adaptable work environments, yet flexible hours and adaptable work environments are rarely found in the workplace. This leaves a large gap in our ability to find joy and resilience.

The opportunity to connect the importance of joy and resilience with effective mechanisms for support at work makes the intangible tangible. It starts with identifying how joy leads to better overall performance and job satisfaction. Leaders in the workplace are constantly looking for data to support any risk before changing the status quo. Employees recognize the importance of joy and the positive effects it has on their professional lives. An opportunity to justify making the needed changes within organizations arrives only when leaders recognize that the well-being of their employees directly impacts productivity in the workplace.

A supportive work environment is essential in finding joy and building resilience. It's vital for leaders to demonstrate commitment to this goal by providing their employees with access to resources and support systems, such as resilience training programs. As with our Keane Insights' self-paced eLearning program called "Growing Your Resilience: Navigating Stress and Change at Work and in Life," these types of trainings substantially enhance an employee's capacity to manage stress and sustain their well-being. Leaders can also enhance their own resilience by fostering a deeper connection to the essence of who they are, which allows them to navigate challenges with greater clarity and calm. In turn this helps them maintain their mental equilibrium and promote a balanced approach to stress management, crucial skills for leaders if they want to bring more positive energy into the workplace.

The ability to sustain resilience and effectively manage stress often means the difference between success and failure. Being able to transcend our immediate stressors and access a higher state of awareness provides us with a broader perspective on problems and energizes us mentally and physically, reducing the physiological impacts of stress. The goal is to regularly practice ways to cultivate a sustained sense of inner peace and resilience, which is vital for making sound decisions and leading effectively in high-pressure environments.

AREAS OF RESILIENCE

Before we get to the building blocks of resilience, let's talk a little bit about context. Resilience can apply to individuals, groups, and organizations.

Resilience in Context

Individuals	Groups	Organizations
Personal skills and resources to withstand pressure and stress	A family or community group pulls together to move through a stressful event	Deal with change and stress without making decisions that harm the long-term success of the company

1. Individual resilience is something we've talked about a bit already, and you're likely intimately familiar with it. In a nutshell, individual resilience is about having the personal skills and resources to withstand pressure and stress, then returning to an equilibrium (or better) when the stress has passed. This involves developing coping strategies, emotional regulation, and a positive outlook. Practicing mindfulness, maintaining physical health through exercise, and seeking social support are all ways to enhance personal resilience. By cultivating these skills, individuals can manage their reactions to stress more effectively and recover from setbacks with greater ease.

Through my interviews with experts across industries, I've discovered that many have systems or rituals to start their days. When I spoke with two-time Olympian Pedrya Seymour, I asked her whether there were things she does that get her into the right mindset and give her the energy she needs to be resilient. Her response was that it's the small things that bring her joy:

> A couple years ago, I wrote down the little things that make me happy. I wrote down trying a new coffee shop, trying a new restaurant, just small things like having a slow morning [and] going to the beach. Those simple things made me happy. So after practice, I would go and do those things, and that kept a balance. So, I understood that track was my job, or is my job, but I still had to find something outside of that.

Reflecting on Seymour's story, I realize I also have a morning routine that energizes me. My day begins with spiritual practices, including various prayers and meditations. I then journal about what's happening in my life, recent wins, my feelings, what I'm grateful for, my goals, any obstacles, and what brings me the most joy. Finally, I make and enjoy a cup of hot chai tea before diving into my important tasks for the day.

Whatever it is that helps you stay resilient as an individual, do it. As long as you're not hurting or harming anyone, it's okay to take care of yourself. That individual resilience will go a long way in helping you stay resilient in groups and at work.

2. Group resilience includes families and communities. A resilient family or community is one that can effectively utilize its internal resources to maintain connection and well-being during difficult times. For example, a resilient family facing a severe illness or a financial setback can lean on each other for support, growing closer and stronger through adversity rather than the opposite. A resilient family communicates openly, supports each other, and works together to solve problems. This collective strength helps them navigate tough times, ensuring that each member feels supported and understood. Shared experiences and mutual support can lead to stronger family bonds and a more resilient family unit.

When I spoke with John Register, who is one of my mentors in the speaking industry, I was intrigued by his ability to take something traumatic and turn it into something positive in his family life while fulfilling his professional passion with renewed joy. You see, in 1988 and again in 1992, Register qualified for the Olympic trials and was on the path to compete as a member of the 1996 Summer Olympic Team in hurdles. However, in 1994, he hyperextended his knee while leaping over a hurdle, which ultimately led to an amputation of his leg. He now walks with the use of a prosthetic leg. During our interview, he mentioned that family was what helped him stay resilient:

> When I had my accident, one of my fears was that Alice might leave me. So many couples break up from combat; the service member comes back home and [there's] too much of a gap. I saw a lot of that, so I thought maybe that might be my lot, that she's gonna leave me, but that really wasn't my fear. My fear was, "Am I still desirable? How do people want to see me now?" My fear was that I'm not going to be accepted. It was my wife, Alice, who said we're gonna get through this together, and then this became just our new normal—the baseline of my entire existence.

The amazing thing is that Register used his resilience not only to walk and even run again but to recapture his passion and joy for the sport. He went on to win a silver medal in the long jump at the 2000 Paralympic Games, making history by setting the record for America in the long jump, proving that joy aids in resilience, and resilience leads to success.

3. Organizational resilience is surprisingly similar to the other two areas of resilience in that resilient organizations

recognize that moving through change with their best people engaged and making intelligent decisions is doing something worthwhile. Resilient organizations are those that create a positive work environment, foster an organizational culture of open communication, and ensure that employees feel valued and supported. During a corporate restructuring, for instance, a resilient organization might provide additional training and support to its employees, encouraging them to adapt to new roles and responsibilities. This helps the organization survive the immediate challenge and also positions it for future growth and success.

When I spoke with Dr. Taft Parsons III, he discussed how his organization aided him as he became the enterprise medical director of Behavioral Health for Humana Inc., which he noted is "the equivalent of being the CEO of a hospital." I was fascinated by Parsons's ability to overcome stress by using the support of his surroundings and the culture of his organization:

> The biggest mitigating factor for me is I had done my residency there and worked as staff there. It was a workplace where a lot of the staff kind of saw me grow up as a professional and then as a leader. They really, really, really looked out for me. Because they knew me when I was still a trainee, they were very vested in me being successful. It's a very urban hospital with a diverse employee workforce. I think that they were very invested in having me, a Black male, be very successful in

that position. They worked really hard to help me, and that helped quite a bit with mitigating some of that stress with the responsibility.

Whether individual, group, or organizational, resilience involves recognizing stressors, adapting to changes, and using available resources to overcome adversity. By building this resilience, we can better handle pressure, support each other through tough times, and ultimately thrive in the face of challenges.

TYPES OF RESILIENCE

In addition to the different areas of resilience, there are many different types of resilience. Most fall into one of two categories: internal and external. Within those two categories, I've identified eight primary types: (1) spiritual, (2) intellectual, (3) emotional, (4) physical, (5) social, which includes marital, and communal, (6) professional (7) lifestyle, and (8) financial. Building insight, awareness, and capacity in any of these types of resilience can help us get to a place of joy and beyond in all areas of life.

Internal resilience is something we have more control over, while external resilience is something we have less control over. However, each type of resilience is an interplay between the two categories, and each impact us individually, within groups, and inside organizations. Let's start with what we have more control over.

INTERNAL RESILIENCE

Internal resilience is about cultivating a positive mindset, developing emotional regulation, and honing problem-solving skills. For example, practicing gratitude, setting realistic goals, and engaging in regular self-care activities such as exercise, meditation, prayer, or hobbies can significantly boost our internal resilience. By focusing on what we can control, we build a foundation that helps us navigate stress more effectively.

1. SPIRITUAL RESILIENCE

Spiritual resilience is the ability to maintain a clear sense of purpose, values, and self-identity despite adversity. It involves unwavering commitment to core beliefs and a deep understanding of one's purpose. This resilience fosters inner strength and peace, allowing individuals to navigate challenges and find meaning in their experiences.

When I spoke with Liza Rossi about this, she emphasized that spiritual practices are vital in maintaining this type of resilience because they enable us to rise above stress and adversity with a clear and centered mind: "For me, spiritual resilience is rooted in the daily practices that help me tap into my inner strength. It's about finding those golden nuggets of growth and understanding, even in the most challenging situations."

Mercedes Martin also underscores the significance of spiritual resilience through intentional actions and rituals. She spends at least one day a week mostly in silence, which allows her time for reflection and connection with her inner self. Martin highlights the importance of maintaining a balance between mind, body, and spirit, emphasizing that a spiritual mindset fosters an understanding of our interconnectedness. By integrating spirituality into her routine, she cultivates resilience, which fortifies her internally and enhances her leadership capabilities. This holistic approach to resilience is particularly resonant with individuals in diverse cultural contexts, reinforcing the importance of spirituality in authentic and sustainable leadership.

Serin Oh's journey is similar. During her darkest times, Oh found herself stripped of everything she once identified with, leading her to delve deeply into her faith. This exploration allowed her to build her identity on the belief that she was created with purpose by a loving God. "For me, just being authentic to who I am, surrendering to the plan that God has for me, really shaped my life so far into something that I've never imagined." By seeing herself and others as meticulously crafted masterpieces, Oh learned to love herself and others genuinely. Her faith provided a solid foundation, enhancing her resilience and enabling her to navigate life's challenges with a sense of purpose and joy. Her journey illustrates how spiritual resilience can profoundly fortify internal resilience.

2. INTELLECTUAL RESILIENCE

Intellectual resilience is the capacity to undertake challenges head-on while focusing on solutions and maintaining progress towards specific goals and a future vision. It involves adaptability, problem-solving, and a commitment to personal growth.

Bruce Turkel exemplifies intellectual resilience through his commitment to continual learning. As the founder of Turkel Brands, he has helped leaders and companies navigate the complexities of modern consumer expectations, emphasizing the importance of knowing who you are and what you want to achieve: "You have the responsibility of knowing what that is. And that takes work." By conducting interviews and analyzing commonalities, Turkel has discovered that living authentically requires introspection and setting realistic yet challenging goals. His approach to running marathons illustrates this type of resilience, as he focuses on personal improvement and therapeutic benefits rather than external validation: "I knew I had to do all the training. I couldn't just show up and then go run and finish it."

Dr. Thomas RaShad Easley, founder of Mind Heart for Diversity Consulting, demonstrates intellectual resilience through his diverse experiences and leadership roles. As inaugural Assistant Dean of Community and Inclusion at both Yale University and North Carolina State University, Dr. Easley has dedicated himself to fostering equitable work cultures. He states, "You have to do both: shift how the organization looks and how it operates." This dual focus on diversity and operational change underscores Dr. Easley's commitment to equity and inclusion. Combined with his commitment to personal growth and adaptability, Easley shows us the value of self-reliance and continuous self-improvement in overcoming professional and personal challenges.

3. EMOTIONAL RESILIENCE

Emotional resilience is the ability to maintain a positive outlook, or even find humor, in difficult situations. It involves effectively managing and overcoming feelings of sadness, nervousness, and stress to ensure overall emotional well-being.

Dr. Taft Parsons III captures emotional resilience through his leadership in the healthcare sector. His journey from practicing psychiatrist to an administrative leader, a role in which he oversees Aetna's psychiatrists and directs CVS Health's behavioral health strategy, showcases his adaptability and capacity for handling complex, high-pressure situations. Dr. Parsons emphasizes the importance of being open to new opportunities and managing stress through practical strategies: "Getting comfortable with discomfort makes transitions in life and taking new opportunities much easier." His ability to empathize with others' perspectives and set reasonable limits further highlights his emotional resilience. "Being better at setting reasonable limits helps a lot with stress and being overwhelmed," he advises.

Nadia Turner embodies emotional resilience by blending her creativity and empathy with her professional expertise. Her background in music and entertainment enriches her therapeutic approach, offering innovative and expressive techniques that demonstrate her unwavering dedication to the well-being of her clients as well as herself. Turner's journey from *American Idol* finalist to mental health advocate highlights her ability to overcome challenges and leverage her experiences for personal growth. "Joy is everything," she says, highlighting the importance of fighting for and maintaining joy despite life's obstacles. Her commitment to integrating music therapy into her practice showcases the profound impact of combining passions to foster healing and resilience. "I fight for joy," she asserts, "and I'm not letting it go."

4. PHYSICAL RESILIENCE

Physical resilience is about maintaining good health to the point at which we rarely experience common ailments such as headaches or digestive issues. It includes getting six to eight hours of sleep nightly and feeling alert throughout the day. Achieving this often requires a specific mindset that's focused on health and well-being.

Pedrya Seymour's journey from the beautiful islands of the Bahamas, to become a two-time Olympian is a testament to physical resilience. Her dedication to representing her country in the 100-meter hurdles at both the 2016 Rio and 2020 Tokyo Olympics highlights her ability to push her body to its limits. Despite facing personal and professional challenges while grieving the loss of her brother in the middle of her track season, Seymour remained focused by leveraging her disciplined upbringing and strong support system to excel both on and off the track. "Resilience means going through stuff but coming out better," she explains, emphasizing the importance of mental and emotional strength in achieving physical feats. Her story underscores the significance of maintaining a positive mindset and finding joy in small, everyday moments, which ultimately fuel her resilience.

John Register's inspiring journey from being an Olympic hopeful to a Paralympic silver medalist epitomizes physical resilience. After his devastating injury, Register harnessed his internal resilience to overcome societal stigmas and personal fears. With unwavering support from his wife, Alice, and a strong faith in God, he chose to view his prosthetic leg not as a limitation but as a means to pursue new athletic goals. "I did not overcome the loss of my limb," he explains. "To overcome the loss would mean I'd have to grow it back. What I overcame were the limits I placed on myself and that others placed on me." Register's story of transitioning from Olympic trials to earning a silver medal at the 2000 Paralympic Games illustrates the power of mindset and determination in achieving remarkable physical feats.

EXTERNAL RESILIENCE

External resilience encompasses the environmental and support systems that surround us. This category consists of the types of resilience that are strengthened by the relationships we cultivate and the environments in which we operate. For corporate leaders and entrepreneurs, this means leveraging a robust network of family, friends, and professional contacts to access vital resources such as healthcare, education, and a supportive workplace culture. These external factors significantly influence our ability to manage stress and recover from setbacks, but they're also the ones we have less control over, so we must use our internal resilience in tandem.

5. SOCIAL RESILIENCE

Social resilience is about having close, secure relationships that help support us. In the workplace, it involves spending quality time with others outside of work, knowing where to turn for support, and maintaining positive working relationships with colleagues. This encompasses community involvement and philanthropy as well as fostering connections that enhance marital, parental, and communal resilience.

Marital resilience has a focus on building and maintaining a close and secure relationship with a spouse, including spending quality time together and knowing where to turn for support. Finesse Mitchell has exemplified external resilience throughout his career and found the value in marital resilience. His success is a result of not only his talent and determination but also the support systems he has cultivated. During our interview, Mitchell, who is also an experienced dating advice columnist for *Essence*, emphasized the significance of having a strong support system at home: "Who you attach yourself to is the most important decision you can make. You have to attach yourself to somebody who believes in that goal one thousand percent." He warns entrepreneurs that whomever they marry significantly impacts their journey, highlighting that marital support plays a vital role in achieving professional and personal goals.

Parental resilience involves developing close, secure relationships with our children, including spending quality time with them and being their support system. Nikki Spoelstra is a single mother of three who personifies parental resilience by navigating tough life experiences with ferocity and poise. Her background as a former inner-city middle school educator, championship-winning dance team coach, and Miami HEAT Dancer reflects her diverse skills and resilience. She offers profound insights through the metaphor of a snow globe: Even when it gets shaken up, the little figurines don't move. She uses that metaphor to reflect on the importance of staying rooted amid chaos, saying, "What a beautiful thing to teach our kids to shake the snow globe. Like shake it up, baby, shake it up. You know, this is you; you stay still, you stay stoic, you stay proud. You stay rooted when there's noise and chaos around you." Communication is everything, and yes, it is okay to discuss sensitive issues with our children and young adults. It's also a blessing when they open up about their feelings.

Communal resilience is about fostering close, secure relationships within the community, including spending quality time with others outside of work and strengthening our social network. It's a type of resilience that's strengthened through supportive environments and networks, and enhanced through nurturing connections and relationships in which gaining buy-in from those around you is crucial. As Liza Rossi shared, "In my experience, communal resilience is most important because it's not just about tangible support, it's about a deeper, spiritual buy-in. When people truly understand the energy and authenticity behind what you do, their support becomes more meaningful and impactful." Rossi further emphasized that when communities are engaged at this deeper level, it enhances the effectiveness of any initiative: "When people feel the joy and passion behind your work, it influences their decision-making in powerful ways." This spiritual connection and authentic engagement within the community are what truly drive success and resilience, making communal support an invaluable asset.

6. PROFESSIONAL RESILIENCE

Professional resilience is a key aspect of external resilience that involves harnessing environmental resources and support systems to navigate and thrive in vocational settings. This type of resilience enables us to successfully adapt to challenges and changes in our careers, and it helps us enjoy our work and maintain positive interactions with colleagues and others in the professional environment.

Nadya Maree, a professional counselor with over 15 years of experience, showcases the value of professional resilience through her practice of developing robust support networks: "The practice of developing support networks has allowed me to seek out opportunities that have been shared with me by others, opportunities that I might not have sought out for myself." By focusing on positive outcomes and future goals despite current failures or setbacks, Maree underscores the importance of leveraging connections with family, friends, and professional contacts, as well as accessing resources such as healthcare and supportive workplace cultures. This comprehensive approach significantly enhances her ability to manage stress and recover from professional challenges.

Finesse Mitchell's journey in comedy and entertainment also showcases professional resilience. Transitioning from college life to the comedy scene in 1999, he made his mark with appearances on BET's *Comic View* and later *Saturday Night Live*. He expresses gratitude for his humble beginnings: "Thank God for people who were genuinely shocked, saying, 'I didn't know Finesse could do this.' They were really laughing, whether with me or at me, they were just laughing, thinking, 'This dude is funny.' It was the beginning of my comedy career, nurtured in an insulated place where people knew me and I knew some inside jokes." Mitchell's success is rooted in leveraging a robust network of support systems, from his fraternity brothers to industry mentors and peers. "Surround yourself with like-minded people or with people who won't discourage you," he advises.

7. LIFESTYLE RESILIENCE

Lifestyle resilience refers to maintaining a healthy balance between work and personal life by making time for hobbies and personal interests. It involves incorporating enjoyable activities into daily routines to ensure overall well-being and fulfillment.

Elizabeth Davis epitomizes lifestyle resilience through her diverse experiences and commitment to helping others. Her journey is marked by her dedication to seniors, her strategic acumen, and her active involvement in community service. A former Miami Dolphins Cheerleader, Davis has a background in cheer and dance, which has also played a significant role in shaping her resilience: "Being a dancer and cheerleader taught me the importance of teamwork, discipline, and performing under pressure." These experiences have provided a foundation for her professional success and enriched her personal life as well. Davis demonstrates that lifestyle resilience is about leveraging extracurricular activities and community involvement to build a strong support network, maintain balance, and enhance well-being.

Serin Oh's journey beautifully illustrates the concept of external resilience through lifestyle pursuits. Her story demonstrates how lifestyle activities, such as music and performance, can create a support system that fosters resilience: "My artists' journey started in the year of social distancing. I had the opportunity to perform among a lineup of major K-pop artists, and Joy Ruckus Club's festival was about celebrating Asian American artists across the world." This network of festivals and international performances provided Oh with a platform to thrive despite challenges. When you listen to her music, you hear joy and resilience intertwined.

8. FINANCIAL RESILIENCE

Financial resilience is a key aspect of external resilience, particularly for leaders and entrepreneurs, because it's about having well-managed finances and a clear understanding of income and expenses. It involves having sufficient resources to withstand financial impacts, such as job loss, until new opportunities arise and the financial stability to withstand economic challenges and uncertainties. This includes maintaining a diversified income stream, building an emergency fund, and making informed financial decisions. A report from Aflac notes, perhaps unsurprisingly, that the groups with the most financial struggles are the ones that exhibit the most burnout symptoms.[30] By ensuring financial resilience, we can better navigate business fluctuations and personal financial stress, thereby enhancing our overall capacity to cope with adversity.

Kelvin McLaurin exhibits this principle through his disciplined approach to budgeting and saving. With over 30 years of experience leading enterprise-level transformations across multiple industries, McLaurin has consistently emphasized living within one's means: "I've always lived my life well within my means. It doesn't matter what you make, but living within your means allows you to weather any storm." His financial strategy includes paying tithes, making significant charitable donations, and allocating a substantial portion of his income to savings, resulting in a sustainable and balanced lifestyle. This approach both fosters his personal financial security and demonstrates the importance of strategic financial planning in building external resilience. "If you do things right, you'll be able to live the way you live off of that," McLaurin asserts, highlighting how meticulous financial management can provide a robust foundation for navigating life's uncertainties.

Josh Landay also embodies this concept by combining creativity and analytics to drive his organization's mission and personal financial stability. "I thrive when I can harness both sides of my brain to solve complex problems," he shared during our interview. This balance of skills is crucial in his role at Gifted Savings, an organization that provides direct investments to high school students, empowering them to achieve their dreams. Landay reflected on the impact of the organization's work, sharing that it's amazing to see a student beam with pride knowing that someone believes enough in them to gift investments: "Our hypothesis is that it increases their confidence in themselves and their ability to do hard things, reducing anxiety about their financial situation." By leveraging his diverse skills and strong support systems, Landay demonstrates how financial resilience can be cultivated and sustained through strategic and thoughtful actions.

Each of the eight types of resilience impact us individually, within groups, and inside organizations. Individually, resilience helps us manage personal stressors and challenges. In groups, like families or communities, resilience allows us to support each other and work together to overcome collective challenges. Within organizations, resilience helps create a supportive culture that can withstand and adapt to changes and stressors. By understanding and developing both internal and external resilience, we can create a holistic approach to managing stress and fostering growth in all areas of life.

WHERE ARE YOU ON YOUR RESILIENCE JOURNEY?

In part 2, you'll be exploring in detail the three stages of a resilience journey. Before doing that, take this opportunity to preassess your current level of resilience:

➤ What core values define you and guide you in your decision-making during challenging times?

➤ What strategies do you use to overcome a challenge and demonstrate your resilience?

➤ How do you respond to unexpected setbacks and stay focused and motivated?

➤ How do you encourage and foster resilience within yourself, your family, and your organization or team?

➤ How do you handle criticism and feedback? What steps do you take to turn it into a growth opportunity?

➤ What techniques do you use to manage your most significant source of stress effectively?

➤ How do you stay adaptable in the face of change? What practices help you embrace new challenges?

➤ What personal and professional goals drive you, and how do they align with your resilience-building efforts?

KEANE INSIGHT: One of the best and easiest ways to build resilience is to treat yourself to short breaks throughout your workday. Take a little time for self-care! I call it the "turtle approach": creating a space where you can enjoy doing the things you like to do. Slow and steady wins the race. Sometimes that 10- to 15-minute break gives us the energy to be resilient and cope with the many other pressing priorities in our lives.

You've discovered that stress is a natural response to various challenges or demands, that it manifests in two main forms, and that there are eight types of resilience encompassing internal and external resilience. The impact of stress is far-reaching. It can affect us physically through symptoms such as headaches and muscle tension, emotionally by causing anxiety and depression, and behaviorally by disrupting sleep and appetite patterns. Recognizing these impacts of stress helps us effectively manage and mitigate its effects.

You've also gained insight into the crucial concept of resilience, which is the capacity to adapt and recover from adversity. Resilience is fundamental in maintaining joy despite stress, as joy fosters positive emotions that can buffer against the detrimental effects of stress. Practical activities including mindfulness, regular physical exercise, and nurturing social connections have been highlighted as effective ways to build resilience. This concept extends beyond individuals to groups and organizations, emphasizing the importance of both internal strengths and external support systems. Understanding and implementing these resilience-building strategies can enhance your ability to thrive and find joy even in the face of stress, ensuring personal and collective well-being.

Now that you have a firm grasp of the importance of joy and resilience and how to find them amid stress, let's move on to building resilience in yourself and promoting it in others.

eLearning Training

A self-paced course to strengthen resilience strategies for individuals, teams, and organizations. Enhance stress management and well-being while empowering leaders to build self-awareness, navigate challenges with clarity and calm, and promote a balanced, positive workplace culture.

PART 2

THE MODEL

During the time I was discovering my joy in the garden, I thought to myself, *Perhaps I can create more of this, both in my own life and in the lives of others.* I found a blueprint, that formula for joy, and it's a new way of thinking that isn't harsh and strict. I simply did three things to help myself tap into joy as a way to manage stress, stay psychologically flexible, and maintain my drive for success. Those three things became THE 3 STAGES ALONG YOUR RESILIENCE JOURNEY™: Ready, Set, Go.

The 3 Stages Along Your Resilience Journey™

I call the Ready stage "discovering yourself." In this stage, you'll begin to understand yourself through deepening your self-awareness, uncovering your stress triggers, and exploring what brings you peace. Self-awareness is a vital part of this stage, so you'll find out what your stressors are and discover what activities de-stress you and bring you joy. You may find out that you don't even like cake and prefer ice cream.

When you understand yourself, it's time to understand the landscape of where you are, which is the Set stage or what I call "designing your landscape." You'll learn how to navigate the dynamics of your workplace more effectively and foster a positive culture around you. When you identify how to navigate the landscape that you're in, it becomes your time to cook for others and share your cake.

After designing your landscape, you'll be in a place where you can confidently move forward and take action by delivering on your goals. This is the Go stage, or what I call "delivering on your goals," and you'll do this by aligning your goals with proactive actions. This will allow you to take charge of your destiny with renewed vigor.

When everything is in alignment, you'll begin to have more of a sense of control of your destiny and your outward circumstances. You'll create a resilient life of your own design. Because that design will help you navigate your personal life, it will also equip you to work through changes and challenges you might face in the workplace. With a growth mindset, you'll have the energy to face stress, with all its twists and turns, all the while being able to make an impact and influence change.

Now let's start discovering.

CHAPTER 4

DISCOVERING YOURSELF

How does a yeti build his house?
Igloos it together.

~John Brueckner, *World's Greatest Dad Jokes*

The first step in growing through resilience is to discover what brings us joy. When I spoke with Dr. Easley about how he goes about this, he had this advice:

> Get quiet. Try to cancel out all the noise in your life because if you're feeling burned out, it's probably because you're burning at both ends. So what we have to do is cancel the noise out. Because the more noise you hear, the more you move to the noise. If you can cancel the noise out . . . you can probably slow down and get it quiet, and then if you can't handle the quiet, you already know what your first issue is: You haven't accepted yourself. See if you can sit quietly on your own, just with yourself.

If you can't think of activities that you enjoy or can't remember the last time you did any of them or even sat with yourself, that's okay. We've all been there. When we give so much to everyone else, there just doesn't seem to be enough left for ourselves. But I can't stress enough the importance of being aware of when we need to reconnect with ourselves. Consider this your wake-up call and start doing something for yourself.

INVESTIGATION

Discovering yourself is about more than just knowing what you like and don't like. It's about understanding what lights you up, what makes you authentically you and truly joyful. It's about doing the internal work so that you can not only survive but thrive. Let's start by assessing where you are:

- What activities or projects bring you the most joy? How do they do this?

- When was the last time you felt truly joyful and fulfilled? What were you doing? What were you thinking?

- What are your top three core values in work and life?

- What are you naturally good at, and how do these strengths help you as a leader?

- When was a time you felt a deep sense of satisfaction as a leader? What contributed to that feeling?

- What makes it special when you have a positive interaction with a team member?

- How do you incorporate mindfulness and relaxation into your routine to enhance your effectiveness as a leader?

- What are some of the things you're noticing in your business or your industry right now that are adding stress that wasn't there two to three years ago?

- What three things are you grateful for? How do they impact your leadership and team culture?

- What three goals do you have, either for your life or your work? What steps will you take to move closer to your aspirations and bring more joy into your life and role at work?

- Who can support you on this journey of self-discovery and joy?

ESSENTIAL ELEMENTS FOR DEVELOPING RESILIENCY

To grow our resilience, we need three key factors: (1) a growth mindset, (2) psychological flexibility, and (3) self-awareness. These three components are crucial after assessing our current state, discovering our joys and what truly lights us up, and recognizing what makes us authentically ourselves. Engaging in this internal work empowers us to navigate challenges with confidence and adaptability. By nurturing these qualities, we can build a strong foundation for personal and professional growth, ensuring a resilient and fulfilling life.

1. GROWTH MINDSET

Harvard Business Review found that "Succeeding as a top leader has little to do with your title and everything to do with your mindset."[31] It's about the way we think and the ability to expand our self-awareness. Whether we perceive something as a success or a failure, good or bad, the way we set our minds affects our resiliency in our lives and careers. Kelvin McLaurin's journey vividly illustrates this principle. Reflecting on his upbringing, he shared, "That whole mindset around controlling what you can control came out because, believe me, I couldn't control much growing up." This mindset both helped McLaurin succeed in challenging environments and taught him the importance of focusing on what he could influence and letting go of what he couldn't.

Generally speaking, people with a fixed mindset tend to view their abilities as unchangeable and struggle to bounce back from setbacks; they easily lose motivation and tend to retreat. When you're in a fixed mindset, you're condensed, closed off from entertaining new ways of doing things, and you stay stagnant. You're less likely to grow because there isn't enough energy in you to nurture your mind to help it grow and expand. Those with a growth mindset are more resilient because they believe in the potential for improvement and have a willingness to put in effort and adapt to change; they welcome expansion and creative thinking.

Have you ever played golf? Golf is truly a game of the mind. When I play, my mindset determines how and where I hit the ball. If my thinking is clear, my body is positioned correctly and relaxed. I first look to where I want to hit the ball, then I keep my eye on the ball and trust the process of the full swing to the finish, all the while imagining myself in a bubble. This allows me to block out the noise and focus. Then I swing.

But the work itself was not done at that moment; that was just the follow-through. The work was done when I set my mind to discovering my joy in the game, then learning to swing with precision to get the ball where I wanted it to go. It was my mindset that allowed me to do that.

As in the game of golf, what we envision becomes the game we play. Resilience isn't just about how strong we are, how long we've been working at something, or how well we've

powered through our challenges. It's about our mindset. Tiger Woods, who's at the top of his game, steps onto the course believing he has already won. Likewise, on our journey of building resilience, we need to be proactive in adapting our mindset.

During our interview, Nikki Spoelstra and I talked a lot about the critical importance of having the right mindset. While she understands that we're all "susceptible to falling into the darkness of the cards [we're] dealt because [sometimes] they're scary, hard, and traumatic," she notes, "There's a point in time when each of us must make a decision about what we're going to do with our circumstances and how we're going to live our lives." For Spoelstra, this means resetting our autopilot mode: "People need to set a foundation for what their autopilot is going to look like. Is your autopilot going to look like you falling apart, making bad decisions, and resorting to unhealthy ways of coping, or is it going to look like something that's helpful in healing and self-care?"

Spoelstra's approach to resilience started with discovering herself and what she values most, which is peace and happiness. Then she started building her landscape on that foundation, setting a preventative approach that allowed her to be ready with the right mindset when crises showed up in her life. She could trust her autopilot to take her where she needed to go. And when she looks back at it, she can see how all the pieces—joy, stress, resilience, and Ready, Set, Go—fit together.

If you don't have a solid foundation yet, that's okay. In the next chapter, we'll be discovering how you can start using a growth mindset to design your landscape. That way, you'll be ready and know how to respond when inevitable challenges and changes come your way. But before moving on, take a moment to think about how you look at stressful situations.

Stress often traps us in a fixed mindset. What intensifies this stress is how we frame the moments in our day, including our perceptions of success and the narratives we create in our minds. By adopting a growth mindset and seeing challenges as opportunities for transformation, we can reframe our experiences, reduce stress, and find new ways to nurture ourselves and thrive.

Nature understands this, and life often mimics nature. I like to think about this while sitting by my window, savoring a hot cup of tea on a morning after the rain. I gaze at the papaya tree I planted a few months ago. Frequent, brief showers are common in Florida, and they've helped the tree flourish, yet I notice the yellow, dying leaves at the base of the tree. I remind myself that as the tree grows, it sheds what is no longer useful in its current form. The fallen leaves transform, nurturing the tree as they decompose into fertilizer. This realization shifted my perspective as a gardener, teaching me that letting go is a natural part of growth.

Whatever our stressors are, whether money, time, technology, or getting along with people at work, it all starts with a shift in the way we think. When we discern what's causing us that feeling of unease, we can begin to determine what's in our span of control. Only then can we take the next steps.

2. PSYCHOLOGICAL FLEXIBILITY

When flexing our resilience muscles, the most important thing we can do is remain psychologically flexible. The flexible approach to resilience is about springing back into shape after a change or a challenge, like that rubber band I mentioned before. Psychological flexibility involves four distinct skills:

1. The ability to adapt to fluctuating demands
2. The understanding of how to reconfigure mental resources
3. The capacity to shift perspectives
4. The capability to balance competing demands

The thing is, most of us actually know how to do these things already and are actually pretty good at them, just not when we're stressed.

What helps is setting realistic goals, those that matter to us and have a clear sense of purpose. Then we need to organize and prioritize our tasks through time management strategies, including taking breaks. In the process, we must remain flexible enough to approach problems from different perspectives as well as balance competing demands from personal and professional life through planning, delegation, and self-care routines. This psychological flexibility ensures stability and prevents burnout, and it is key for maintaining focus and productivity. We must embrace change as an opportunity for growth.

Nicole Hunt holds a master's degree in social work and has more than 14 years of experience in the healthcare sector, including at Aetna and CVS Health. When I met with her, she reinforced the idea of embracing change to stay resilient: "Knowing who I am and how I add value has helped me navigate the constant change in my workplace by feeling certain that there will always be another opportunity for me and that I'll land where I should in the work world." Psychological flexibility is integral to adapting and thriving amid change, and it starts with self-awareness.

5. SELF-AWARENESS

Self-awareness is a vital step on the path to resilience because it encompasses the way we think, the stories we tell ourselves, and the activities that bring us joy and help us feel refreshed and recharged. It's through self-awareness that we come to the realization that in order to help others, we have to help ourselves first. That's why on airplanes they advise us that if the cabin pressure decreases, we should put an oxygen mask over our own face first before putting one on a child or helping someone else. If we don't take care of ourselves, we may never get to a place where we can help someone else. And to take care of ourselves, we need to be self-aware.

When I asked Spoelstra what actions she took to build the resilience she needed to maintain her foundation of peace and joy, she talked a lot about self-awareness.

> I had to take a moral inventory of myself by looking in the mirror and getting really honest. I had to see everything that was beautiful about me and everything that was really awful about me. And I had to

really acknowledge that I'm beautiful, wonderful, and extraordinary but can also be mean, envious, and dark. Instead of trying to prove that I don't have the capacity to be mean, envious, and judgmental, I had to say, "I don't really want to feel so much envy. I don't want to have to resort to meanness when I'm upset. I don't want to have to feel angry, jealous, hostile, or cruel." I had to discover that I don't like how those behaviors made me feel when I engaged in them.

Now I'm fully capable of coming back to my peace by acknowledging all the facets of who I am and who I'm trying to be and not being so harsh on myself. Mistakes are inevitable, especially when we're overstimulated. But through self-awareness, I built a foundation of peace, which for me is deeply tied to my sense of resilience.

Just as Spoelstra discovered, no one but you can tell you who you are. When you're self-aware, when you can really look at yourself from all different aspects, you can better navigate whatever changes or challenges come along.

While we often throw it around on a whim, self-awareness is a more complex topic than many of us recognize. Take a look at one of the more comprehensive definitions: "Self-awareness consists of a range of components, which can be developed through focus, evaluation and feedback, and provides an individual with an awareness of their internal state (emotions, cognitions, physiological responses) that drives their behaviors (beliefs, values, motivations) and an awareness of how this impacts and influences others."[32] It's huge, isn't it? This definition includes seven primary concepts:

1. Beliefs and values
2. Internal mental state (including feelings, emotions, thoughts, and cognition)
3. Physical sensations or physiological responses
4. Personality traits (including personal assessments of our strengths and weaknesses)
5. Motivations
6. Behaviors
7. Awareness of how others perceive us

It's no wonder so many of us struggle with self-awareness. In fact, although it's a top skill for leaders to have, particularly so they understand how to make informed decisions that impact those they lead as well as their organizations, many leaders lack self-awareness.[33] Without a sense of self-awareness, leaders are left without the vision they need to positively impact the landscape, which often leads to a lack of empathy, hinders their awareness of team dynamics, and weakens team collaboration. Leaders are caught in the middle of needing to drive performance and profitability while being empathetic in the workplace.

Spoelstra's best advice to those who are feeling stressed and burned out to help them grow resilience is simple: "Journal. Writing down your goals and dreams is very important. From there you can create lists and actionable steps for how to get there. It might seem stressful, overwhelming, or counterintuitive, but really you're creating a stepladder for getting to where you want to go." Again, it's the simple things that bring joy, therefore resilience, into our lives.

How do you cultivate self-awareness while leading your life? My big takeaways for doing this are to check in with yourself often (using methods such as journaling and self-reflection) and consider where your strengths and weaknesses lie. For example, perhaps you're great with professional resilience because you're able to withstand a huge amount of pressure and a big workload, but maybe you're not so great with emotional resilience. It helps to always be mindful of ways to chase meaning and joy. By "meaning," I'm referring to the things that really matter to you. And only you can answer that.

Dig deep. Be honest with yourself about what matters, then go after it. You might value being successful in the corporate world and being a connected parent. If so, own it, but have the self-awareness that you're going to need to work hard to find the balance to make both those roles work simultaneously.

EXPLORATION

Now that you have more understanding of the three essential elements of resilience, let's reevaluate where you are.

❖ **Discover Joy Through Self-Care Bingo!**
I've designed an activity to help you prioritize self-care, reduce stress, and enhance your overall joy and well-being.

Using the Self-Care Bingo card, schedule each self-care activity within your chosen timeframe, whether it be a week or a month. As you complete each activity,

The Joyful Leader
SELF-CARE BINGO™

Take 10 Deep Breaths	Learn to Say No	Write in a Journal	Get Plenty of Sleep	Take a Brisk Walk
Seek Out Positive People	Express Gratitude	Meditate	Prioritize Tasks	Read a Good Book
Spend Time with a Loved One	Exercise	**FREE SPACE**	Visualize a Relaxing Scene	De-Clutter Your Office Space
Stretch	Watch Clouds Go By	Hug Someone	Watch a Movie	Take Regular Breaks
Listen to Soothing Music	Enjoy a Hobby	Confront Your Feelings	Talk with a Friend	Dance It Out

mark off the corresponding square on your bingo card. Reflect on how each activity made you feel and journal your thoughts. Once completed, review your journey, celebrate your achievements, and consider how you can integrate these self-care practices into your daily routine for sustained benefits.

You may want to print out a Self-Care Bingo card and put it in a spot you can see every day so that you have a visual reminder to regularly practice self-care.

❖ **Discover Your Stress Triggers**

In what areas of your life are stressful encounters or conflicts taking place? Are your stressors mostly at home or at work? To help you answer these questions, I've designed this Stress Triggers Exercise.

Stress Triggers™

Take a moment to reflect on the things, people, and events that are currently causing you stress. Write down each stress trigger in the corresponding bubble. After completing the exercise, review each of the bubbles and compare them to each other to see where you experience the most stress in your life.

In the center bubble, write down how these stress triggers are affecting you.

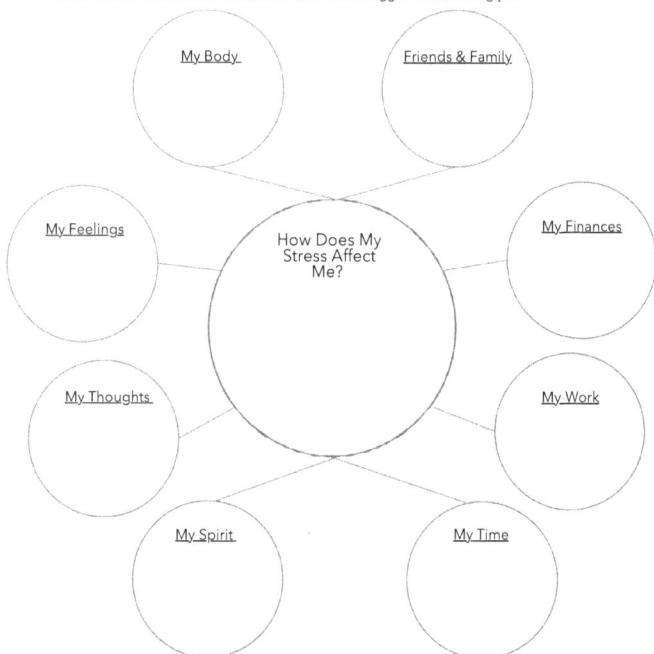

My Body

Friends & Family

My Feelings

How Does My Stress Affect Me?

My Finances

My Thoughts

My Work

My Spirit

My Time

❖ Discover Your Resilience

In which types of resilience are you strongest, and in which are you weakest? To help you determine the answer, I've created this Sphere of Resilience Exercise.

Sphere of Resilience™ Exercise

Use the sphere below to assess each area of your life and find out where you are most resilient and where you can improve. On a scale of 0 to 10, with 10 being the highest possible score, mark down the amount of resilience you have in each area of your life.

Complete the eight spokes of the sphere and compare the amounts in each area, noting where you score higher and where you score lower. Join up the marks to create a circle with your overall results. Does the circle look balanced? Consider the ideal levels for each area and reflect on whether some areas may need attention.

Sphere of Resilience*

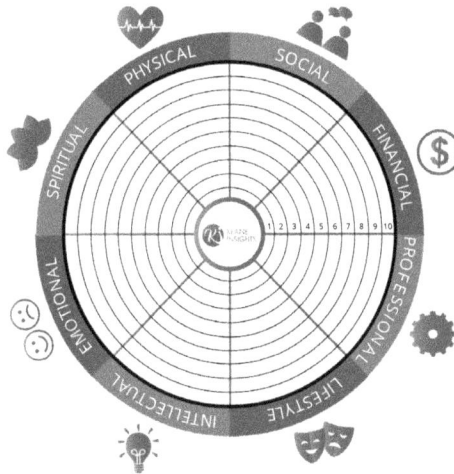

Key Types of Resilience

*Adapted from Paul J. Meyer (1960), Success Motivation Institute®, https://www.mindtools.com/ak6jd6w/the-wheel-of-life

❖ Discover Your Mindset

Give an example of a time when you addressed something with a fixed mindset:

_____

_____

_____

_____

_____

What was the result?

_____

_____

_____

_____

How might a growth mindset have helped you in this situation?

_____

_____

_____

_____

_____

❖ **Discover Your Psychological Flexibility**

To discover your level of psychological flexibility, work through these questions and honestly consider your answers:

➢ How do you typically respond to unexpected challenges or changes in your environment? What strategies do you use to adapt to these situations? Provide an example of a time when you successfully navigated a significant change.

_____

_____

_____

_____

_____

➢ How often do you reflect on your thoughts and emotions during stressful situations? How do you manage these reflections? In what ways have these reflections helped you remain adaptable and open-minded?

_____

_____

_____

_____

_____

➤ When faced with a problem, how do you balance sticking to your initial plan with considering alternative approaches? Can you recall a time when changing your approach led to a better outcome? What factors do you consider when deciding to pivot or persist?

_____

_____

_____

_____

➤ How do you incorporate feedback from others into your decision-making process? Share an instance when feedback led you to change your perspective or actions.

_____

_____

_____

_____

➤ How do you create an environment that encourages open and honest feedback?

_____

_____

_____

_____

➤ In what ways do you practice mindfulness or self-awareness in your daily routine? How does this practice impact your ability to stay flexible and resilient? What specific techniques or exercises do you find particularly effective?

_____

_____

_____

_____

❖ Discover Your Self-Awareness
Identify Your Strengths: Circle All That Apply

Active Listener	Approachable	Artistic	Athletic
Brave	Confident	Cooperative	Creative
Curious	Decisive	Empathetic	Energetic
Enthusiastic	Fair	Fashionable	Flexible
Focused	Forgiving	Good Presenter	Good Time Manager
Grateful	Have Common Sense	Helpful	Honest
Hopeful	Humorous	Independent	Innovative
Kind	Leader	Logical	Loving
Mathematical	Modest	Open Communicator	Open-Minded
Optimistic	Organized	Patient	Persistent
Problem-Solver	Reliable	Self-Controlled	Socially Aware
Spiritual	Supportive	Team Player	Wise

Identify Your Weaknesses: Circle All That Apply

Aggressive	Anxious	Authoritative	Big Spender
Blunt Communicator	Can't Delegate	Can't Say No	Disorganized
Distrustful	Faultfinder	Fearful of Public Speaking	Hyper- or hypo-focused
Hypersensitive	Illogical	Impatient	Inflexible
Insecure	Judgmental	Lack Common Sense	Lack Empathy
Lack Experience	Lack Knowledge	Loud	Micromanager
Miss Deadlines	Over-Multitasker	Oversensitive	Neglectful of Self-Care
Not a Team Player	Not Detail-Oriented	Overthinker	Perfectionist
Pessimistic	Poor Communicator	Poor Data Analyzer	Poor Decision-Maker
Poor Listener	Poor Time Manager	Poor Work–Life Balance	Procrastinator
Quick-Tempered	Self-Critical	Shy	Stubborn
Unfocused	Unforgiving	Unreliable	Workaholic

KEANE INSIGHT: Self-discovery is about understanding yourself and developing self-awareness. Identifying your strengths and weaknesses brings insight into which strategy would work best for you. Take some time to reflect on what you're really good at and where there are opportunities for improvement. This is the foundation for you to start your resilience journey. Just like the best athletes have coaches, you may want to consider working with an executive coach and sharing your journey with them to help you lay out your success plan.

What brings you real joy, what stresses you out, and what helps you build your resilience are questions only you can answer. And you might have to experiment a little to find them. But recognize that to perform at your best, to be resilient and grow through life's inevitable struggles, the truth is you must have joyful activities to tap into as a stress release and to nourish your soul, especially if you want to be more productive at work.

Sometimes the best thing to do is to mind your own business. Focus on yourself. Discover what brings you joy. Get in a bubble—a safe space to be yourself. Do the things you enjoy, not the things forced on you and not the things you're good at but don't bring you joy. If you think about your end goal of bringing more joy and beyond in your life, it gets easier to think about what brings you joy right now. It could be little things, like seeing a sunset or sunrise. (I tend to see more sunsets than sunrises because I'm a night owl.) It could be coloring with your kids, playing board games, playing golf, dancing, running . . . anything at all. All that matters is that you enjoy doing the activity and it ultimately brings you a sense of peace so that you can start building your resilience. When you're feeling that number one stressor in your life, think about this activity to put yourself in a different mindset. Then go schedule it in your calendar for a specific day and time. Don't wait.

Your joy is hiding in places you think you don't have time to find. I encourage you to find them; to slow down and appreciate life. That's what resilience is all about: building yourself up to live your authentic life to its fullest. And I hope in some way I'm helping you do that.

Just remember, you get to write the recipe for your happiness and joy. And if your cake crumbles, you can make a new one by designing your landscape.

Digital Workbook:

Guided exercises and prompts to encourage self-reflection, helping individuals and team deepen their understanding of their strengths, growth areas, and overall resilience.

CHAPTER 5

DESIGNING YOUR LANDSCAPE

What's the best way to carve wood?
Whittle by whittle.

~John Brueckner, *World's Greatest Dad Jokes*

If you don't design your life, someone else will.

Designing your life starts with designing your landscape, meaning identifying how you navigate the culture of your workplace. It's about emotional intelligence, which involves understanding not just yourself but your part in a system, your part in a culture. To do this, you need to pay attention to the landscape of your workplace, which begins by understanding workplace culture. Although sometimes we have little control over how the culture is, we can still map a pathway forward.

Before we dive deeper, let's assess your current understanding of your workplace's culture.

INVESTIGATION

To effectively navigate your professional environment, it's crucial to evaluate the culture of your workplace and your role within it, define your goals clearly, and select strategies for growth that minimize stress. This sets the stage for success in growing resiliency. By understanding your workplace culture, setting adaptable goals, and choosing the right strategies for personal and professional development, you can build a resilient path forward. Reflect on these questions to guide your preassessment:

- How does understanding your workplace culture impact your overall success and satisfaction?
- What criteria will you use to set your goals, and how will you adjust them if your circumstances change?
- What approaches will you adopt to ensure continuous growth and learning while managing stress?

UNDERSTANDING WORKPLACE CULTURE

David J. Friedman, an expert in company culture, defines culture as "the commonly held set of values and principles that shows up in the everyday behaviors of the people."[34] He also notes, "While we all may agree about its significance, understanding the real mechanics of culture and, more importantly, how to create and drive it has always been shrouded in mystery."[35] Add to this the fact that in 2022, the average employee experienced 10 planned enterprise changes, including organizational restructures and culture transformations,[36] and is it any wonder so many of us struggle with the culture of our workplace?

Part of understanding workplace culture means recognizing the underlying values and unwritten rules that drive behavior in your organization. It also involves being attuned to the social dynamics, communication styles, and decision-making processes that define your work environment. By understanding the cultural landscape, you can better anticipate challenges, align your actions with organizational goals, and build stronger relationships with team members.

Emotional intelligence plays a critical role in this stage of the model because it's about being aware of your own emotions and those of others, managing your reactions, and using this awareness to navigate social complexities. Understanding yourself as part of a system means acknowledging how your behavior impacts a group and how that group's behavior influences you. This dual awareness creates a sense of belonging and helps us contribute more effectively to our collective goals. By mastering our landscape, we position ourselves to thrive in a place where we as individuals as well as our organizations can succeed. To do this, we need to pay attention to the environment around us.

Although it may seem we have little control over workplace culture, we *can* map a pathway forward. When we start a new job, we enter a preexisting culture that has been shaped by those who came before us. It takes about three to six months to assess the landscape, especially the dynamics of the team. This period is crucial for understanding established norms, communication styles, and the unwritten rules that govern interactions, which enables us to move forward successfully and with confidence as we continue to design our path.

One thing that helps us release stress during these times is learning how to navigate the path effectively. Doing so gives us a sense of purpose and belonging within a landscape that has already been created and a recognition of our value in the bigger story. By aligning ourselves with the existing narrative, we gain clarity on our role and value in that story, helping us reduce stress that arises from feeling disconnected or out of sync with a team's established rhythm. Often, we feel more stress in the workplace when we haven't really learned how to navigate the landscape and become part of the story rather than directing the narrative ourselves. Taft Parsons III explained how this happened to him:

> As you get into leadership, you become responsible for the culture, but at the same time it takes a long time to change. I came in as a trainee with the culture of the hospital and the folks working there, so I was very intimately knowledgeable of what it was like to begin with. As I transitioned from being a trainee to being staff, [I became] a team leader with that factor. Whether people report to you or not, doctors are seen as leaders within the healthcare system. Moving into that official title and leadership role, you have those things that you see as working really well, and you also have things that you see as needing improvement or stuff that has to change. It really helped me [to be] in it from the beginning and grow up there to know what things needed to be changed quickly and what things needed to kind of slowly develop over time. It was an interesting way for me to get into cultural change and doing intentional work, along with having grown up there and being unintentionally already embodied in the culture.

If you're feeling a little overwhelmed about how to start designing a new path for yourself within your workplace or life in general, Bill Burnett and David Evans, authors of *Designing Your Life: How to Build a Well-Lived, Joyful Life* and founders of the framework by the same name, offer five tips:

1. Be curious
2. Try different things
3. Reframe problems
4. Understand it's a process
5. Ask for help[37]

We're not going to go through each tip in detail, but if you ever feel stuck when trying to create a new way of living and working, the solution can usually be found in one of these points. And if you're really stuck, the answer lies in asking for help.

ASKING FOR HELP

There is magic in working together with other experts on a single goal. In fact, have you heard of the systems approach? We'll expand on it more later, but it's the theory that the whole is greater than the sum of its parts. In other words, we are stronger together. Magic happens when working together because that's when each individual gets to know and like the other and their work. Everyone has something of value to share, so don't assume that you can't benefit someone else in some way.

Sometimes people think they're in a position where all they can do is get help from others, when, in fact, they too bring valuable things to the table. I love it when someone says, "Thank you for helping me and allowing me to pick your brain. Now how can I help you?" I often say, "Well there isn't anything I really need right now, but please pay it forward to someone else."

You better believe I'll reach out to those who offer their support in my times of need, just as I'll be there for others in their times of need. But what happens to a person who's left out and feels isolated? Given that being a part of a group is a rewarding feeling that gives us a sense of connection, what's the opposite feeling? Rejection. And rejection often feels like a threat, a threat that can result in

- reduced cognitive performance
- increased self-defeating behaviors
- reduced prosocial behaviors
- reduced meaning and purpose
- decreased well-being (social anxiety, loneliness, reduced self-esteem).[38]

The effects of social rejection are heavily studied in the neuroscience field, and it's quite a fascinating topic. One study was conducted on a game called "Cyberball," a virtual ball-toss game that's often played to create a situation in which one person feels rejected. A group of subjects begin passing a ball from person to person through a web interface, and after a few rounds, one person is excluded. But this person doesn't know it was planned. The study indicated that the rejected player's brain reacted to the situation with anger or sadness.[39] Tossing a ball in an online game is not so different from tossing ideas around in a business team meeting, whether virtual or in person.

Studies show that the emotional feeling of pain from social exclusion overlaps with physical pain, primarily because both kinds of pain are processed in the same area of the brain.[40] In other words, the brain can't tell the difference between physical pain and social distress. Social distress from rejection can lead to decreased cognitive performance, increased self-defeating behaviors, and overall reduced well-being,[41] and strong social relationships not only enhance survival rates but also reduce mortality risk.[42] All of this highlights the critical nature of social needs to our well-being.

How can employees do their best work when they're in pain? How can you? If your organization is built on people who are in a state of threat, what happens to the business? Can there be any way to grow teamwork and collaboration? Today, the effect of an unhealthy workplace environment on employees is estimated to cost American companies $300 billion a year in poor performance, absenteeism, and health costs,[43] and low employee engagement is estimated to cost $8.9 trillion in lost productivity globally.[44] Finding ways to connect is more important than ever.

BUILDING RELATIONSHIPS

In business, there is an expression: "It's not personal, it's just business." But I don't agree with that. Business *is* personal (just not *too* personal), and it *does* matter whether people trust us and whether they get a chance to know us and become our fans.

A study on happiness at work indicated that the two most prevalent causes of employees having bad days at work are a lack of help and support and a lack of praise or recognition for their work.[45] And Gallup found that organizations with engaged employees outperform those with low employee engagement by 202%, resulting in up to 81% less absenteeism, 64% fewer safety incidences, 43% lower turnover, and 23% higher profitability globally.[46] Facts like these prove that when employees are engaged and joyful, when they're in an environment with a high-performing culture, their organizations save money.

And guess what? When people trust us, they often become our career advocates by speaking highly of us and seeking us out when there are new opportunities or when they need our expertise. And those advocates can lead us to more mentors and even sponsors, as well as continued opportunities to grow and succeed in future endeavors. The bridge towards trust is connection, and it's a beautiful thing. Just ask Josh Landay, who believes in the power of building authentic connections to achieve a unified vision: "I believe in the power of building strong, authentic relationships—with teammates, board members, and partners—to strengthen our pursuit of a clear and unified vision."

Leaders have the power to influence employees towards having more positive days at work simply by building trust and connection through engaging. But not just any type of connection, intentional connection. Increasingly more companies operate with many remote employees, so intentional connection from leadership is vital. And if you can build positivity and fun into the connection, that's the golden ticket.

Many studies indicate that having events or activities such as picnics, employee spotlights, or company-wide challenges are ways to bring people together and connect. I find it's the simple things that bring people together. When I heard of a manager opening his meetings by wishing everyone "Happy National Creative Ice Cream Flavor Day," it brought a smile to my face. That simple act brings connection in a fun and playful way.

It was through making connections that I joined the National Speakers Association and networked with some of the greatest national and international speakers. Then I volunteered as a board member for the Florida Speakers Association, and through that I found a speaking coach and mentor. I reconnected with a former career coach who pushed me to expand my knowledge, and I obtained a couple of certifications from the Society for Human Resource Management. That then led me to become a human resources instructor and a mental health subject matter expert.

The best part is that all of this was within my span of control, and all it took was making connections and asking for help. There are many ways to do this, but I find the most effective is seeking out capable help-givers before you even need them, then building relationships with them. This can be accomplished through networking, volunteering, professional branding, mentorship, and sponsorship.

NETWORKING

Through networking, we can determine the resources that are within our control. The decisions we make on our own and our understanding of how our performance is rated as well as determining our sphere of influence and learning who our allies are (those who win when we win) are all components of networking, which is about building a support system that helps us navigate our landscape. Of course, it's also about having some good people in our corner who we can turn to for help when we really need it.

Over time, I've had the opportunity to mentor several mental health clinicians and help them with networking. Nadya

Maree was one of them, and she shared how my advice helped her during a pivotal moment in her career:

> I know that one of the ways to get there is by taking risks, and that's something you shared with me. So when I had an opportunity where I was asked if I would participate in something, I participated in it. I think a year later, you said to reach out to people and remind them of something that I did for them, that they were a part of. And so I spoke to all of them [and asked], "Hey, do you remember me?" and "Can we schedule 15 minutes on your calendar to talk about this role that I'm interested in?" I really think that went a long way, that feedback and advice, because folks did say, "Oh my gosh, I remember that." And when I finally got my interview, the response was, "I have heard so much about you."

So what's keeping you from networking? For many people, with all the things they have to juggle these days, it's a time factor; somehow, building relationships just doesn't seem that important among all our other priorities. Others think they're wasting time if they're being social and chatting. I think that mentality stops a lot of people from creating relationships. With a fixed mindset, they think things like, *I'm doing my work. I'm busy. Stop coming over to my desk and talking to me.* Or they might say, "I did say I have an open-door policy, but we've got stuff to do." Maybe this is you and you're sitting there rolling your eyes. But you have to honor the fact that at some point, relationships matter.

Have you ever seen someone at work who's always joking, talking, and going out for lunch with people? You know, that person who remembers birthdays and brings in gifts? The one who gets the promotion over someone who keeps their head down and focuses solely on the work at hand? Networking matters.

No, this doesn't mean you need to add tissues in your office and invite everyone in to share all their sad stories (we all know there are people who take things too far and don't understand boundaries). What it does mean is that through networking we can build the relationships that will support us on our path of building resilience.

Networking can be as simple as this:

1. Strike up a conversation with someone.
2. Focus on who they are.
3. Make sure they have a good sense of who you are.
4. Note how to stay connected with them.
5. Determine how you can be helpful to them.

VOLUNTEERING

Another way to build relationships is through volunteering. Sometimes when we're going through hard times, the fastest way out of them is to focus on someone else. That's where volunteering can come into play. Focusing on someone else's issues can be a great way to help take the focus off our own, and that in itself is a form of resilience.

Throughout my journey inside the corporate world, I had to be resilient. Every merger and every acquisition were moments of much change, whether in team dynamics or in personnel. This resulted in the landscape around me constantly changing. But I didn't let that change control me; I found a way to control it by being proactive. I had to discover myself and assess my level of resilience, then design my landscape based on what was in my span of control. And guess what I did? I volunteered whenever there was an opportunity to collaborate with another department, which allowed me to expand my network. Almost immediately, I started to notice opportunities appearing at the right time, and that's when I'd make my move.

Adrienne Nicole echoed this approach when she shared, "I was volunteering with the SLE Lupus Foundation while figuring out how to build my business. Through that, I got my first client—a video project—simply because I had built relationships through volunteering. That's how I leveraged my network." Volunteering not only led to new opportunities for Nicole but helped solidify her business foundation. Her story is a perfect example of how taking the initiative to help others can create unexpected pathways for personal and professional growth.

My best advice is to keep a list of people you'd like to ask for a 15-minute discussion. When you reach out, make sure to have a clear goal in mind to keep the conversation focused and valuable for both of you.

PROFESSIONAL BRANDING

As I continued to make my moves, I kept networking and volunteering to keep growing and elevating my brand. Do you realize you have your own brand? Have you ever thought about what your personal brand is? Have you defined it? How are you showing up to work every day? Part of resiliency is understanding what you value, who you are, and what your brand means to you.

Professional branding isn't just a buzzword in the corporate world. It's essential for small businesses, entrepreneurs, nonprofits, and even sole proprietorships. Every organization, regardless of size, benefits from a strong and authentic brand presence. That's because leadership brands are the collective perception others have of us based on our decisions, words, and actions. Strong leadership brands help leaders communicate most effectively while inspiring confidence and trust in those they want to impact.

When I was developing my brand, I had to consider all these elements and more. Summarizing decades of education, experience, and insight into a single paragraph that truly reflects who I am and what I do was a significant challenge. With the guidance and support of trusted mentors and colleagues, I started with a deep process of discovering myself, then I designed the landscape that positioned me for success. Here's what I designed:

MY BRAND STATEMENT

I am a strategic healthcare executive, an inspirational speaker and connector, and an active board member, advisor, and mentor. I am passionate about helping others navigate change by creating meaningful connections that enhance people and access through inclusivity for healthcare and behavioral health professionals, corporate leadership and HR executives, inclusion and belonging advocates, and community organizations. My limitless mindset empowers others to find resilience and joy by helping them navigate challenges, create meaningful connections that enhance people and access, and promote spiritual harmony and inclusivity. My ability to lead and advise as a board member and professional speaker with over two decades of experience in healthcare, behavioral health, and consumer engagement allows me to excel in enhancing leadership, fostering team resilience, and promoting an inclusive culture.

Think about who you really are, how you want to be, and the way you want others to see you. This self-reflection is crucial for building an authentic personal brand. Your brand should encapsulate your values, strengths, and unique qualities, making it clear to others what you stand for and what you bring to the table.

Effectively develop your brand by seeking out mentors and sponsors who can provide guidance and advocate for you. Mentors offer valuable advice and support, helping us grow and navigate our careers. Sponsors, on the other hand, use their influence to open doors for us, promote our work, and help us achieve our career goals. Sponsorship means having someone who speaks highly of us at the table and in rooms where we may not even be aware of the discussions taking place, ensuring our name and achievements are recognized. Mentors and sponsors are essential to building a strong, impactful personal brand, so let's explore both.

MENTORS

Mentors can have a strong influence on our professional careers. They tend to have a strong work ethic that inspires us to be the best we can be every day. They're people who we look forward to keeping in touch with and we have a strong desire to assist if they ever need anything.

In the process of developing my brand, for example, I somehow became a mentor to many people and had the honor of watching them grow and shine. They took my insights to heart and understood that others needed to know and like them and their work. They gained visibility through volunteering to be on projects of interest, sought out stretch assignments, and worked cross-functionally with different departments. And they learned the power of asking for help when needed. I often told them stories of times I was asked to own a project or lead a team and had no idea where to begin. After some time of reflection, I did what my mom—who's a part of my board of mentors—told me to do: Find people who know how to do what you need and ask them for help. My mentees and I discovered the importance of working together to make a stronger impact.

Of the mental health clinicians I've mentored, all of them were promoted to leadership roles during our time together. One of them, Nicole Hunt, a social worker who values mentorship, expressed that trust in a mentor–mentee relationship is built on consistent support and responsiveness. A mentor fosters a strong sense of trust when they allow the mentee to set the agenda for conversations while they remain readily available and genuinely invested in the mentee's development. This trust is further reinforced when the mentor's actions demonstrate that the relationship is a priority even amid their busy schedule, as well as when their guidance is thoughtful and relevant to the mentee's needs. This highlights the significant impact mentors and experienced colleagues can have on us and demonstrates that guidance and support can greatly advance our career development and contribute to our organizational success.

Mentors have always helped me get to the next level, both in my business and in my life. It's nice having a mentor because they can see what we can't, especially when we're so inside of a problem that we can't see it with clarity. Most of us are pretty good at looking at someone else's relationship and telling them exactly what's wrong, and we need to apply that practice to ourselves. It's important to check in with ourselves and see where we are now and how we're going to get to the next level. Mentors help us do that.

One of my mentors once said to me, "Nicole, you need to think through your career path. You are so diverse in your abilities. You can do anything that is asked, and you get pulled into so many things"—hence my burnout—"you need to think through YOUR career path. What space do you want to be in?" It was at that moment I realized that I'd been saying yes to following everyone else's path and that it was my responsibility to determine the path I wanted to take; no one else could do that for me.

These days, we have access to mentors without even knowing them personally. Our mentors could be from different time periods through reading books, different locations through virtual meetings and listening to podcasts, and different industries through in-person and virtual conferences. The sky is the limit. A mentor doesn't even need to know that they're our mentor. Many times, someone has been my mentor from a distance through reading their social media posts and learning about their thought leadership. When I do finally meet them, I let them know they've been an inspiration and mentor to me simply by being themselves.

Finding your mentors can be as simple as this:

- Reading memoirs of those you admire
- Following thought leaders on social media
- Listening to guests on podcasts
- Watching documentaries
- Asking for advice as needed
- Setting up quarterly meetings

Most of us, if we're lucky, have had someone (maybe more than one person in our work environment) who reached out a hand and lifted us up, gave us advice, or stepped in at that moment of need and helped us. Let's also be someone like that for someone else. Let's be the ones who reach out, who mentor, who stop what we're doing to link arms with someone else even if there's seemingly nothing in it for us.

SPONSORS

Though our mentors can sometimes also be our sponsors, mentors mainly offer us guidance and advice, while sponsors take an active role in our advancement. A sponsor is a senior leader, C-suite executive, or high-level influencer. Success within an organization or industry depends on things beyond our contributions and performance. It's important to have someone who supports us and sponsors us as we move throughout and elevate within an organization. A sponsor is committed to our success.

When I spoke with Nadya Maree, she shared this was indeed the case for her: "I had someone advocate for me for an opportunity, and it was incredibly meaningful. What stood out even more was hearing that the CEO and medical director were informed by housekeeping staff that I should be the director of that department. It wasn't just my boss who supported me; people from other departments spoke up about my fitness for the role based on my personality and work ethic. It really reinforced the importance of treating everyone with respect and kindness."

ADVISORS

Like sponsors, advisors take an active role in our advancement, specifically in helping us design our landscape. They might, for example, offer advice on how to navigate business politics, help position us for promotions, or get an entrepreneur closer to closing a contract. Advisors provide career advice and are extraordinarily helpful, especially when they know and understand what we're trying to accomplish in our careers. An advisor is equipped to speak freely, honestly, and in a way that instills confidence in us.

It's important to take calculated risks with an advisor. Make sure you have a trusted relationship with them before you share all your mistakes, worries, or professional strategies. I remember being brought onto a team that had an outside consultant, an advisor figure, so to speak, who was being let go as I was being brought on. During the transition, he offered his services as an advisory resource. He had many years of experience in the industry and was wonderful at answering questions pertaining to my job and sharing key factors for being successful at it. For some reason, I didn't feel comfortable sharing my concerns with him. Maybe it was because he was sharing all the details of other members of the team to somehow develop trust with me. However, I felt that that information was none of my business, and it actually blocked the development of a trusted relationship. It is crucial to trust your instincts in these matters.

EXPLORATION

Now that you have more understanding of how you can design your landscape and how doing so impacts you and your team, let's reevaluate where you are on your joyful resilience journey.

❖ **Evaluate Your Career Goals**

- What roles at work do you want?

- Who do you want to be?

- What space do you want to be in? / What three tangible areas do you want to land in?

- What skills do you need to work on to get there?

- What skills do you have that would help you get to your desired goals but aren't being utilized?

With these goals in mind, write down a list of people who could potentially be a mentor in helping you achieve them:

1. _____

2. _____

3. _____

4. _____

5. _____

❖ **Identify Your Areas of Support**

How do you seek support from your network, and what role does your community play in your resilience?

_____

_____

_____

_____

❖ **Consider Your Well-Being**

How can your employer better support your well-being practices to enhance your joy and resilience?

● Provide flexible working hours

● Offer wellness programs and resources

● Create a supportive and understanding work environment

● Encourage regular breaks and time off

● Other: _____

❖ **Write to a Future Mentor**

Write a short paragraph to someone expressing that you'd like them to be your mentor. Keep these points in mind:

● Show gratitude—thank them for the great advice they've given you thus far in your career.

● Ask for what you want—determine whether they're willing and able to act as a mentor.

● Share expectations—reinforce your current relationship and future needs.

Here's an example: "I really appreciate the great advice you've given me thus far in my career, and I think you could be extraordinarily helpful as I navigate these next couple of years. Would you be willing and available to help me as needed and act as a mentor? I believe you know me very well, understand conceptually what I'm trying to accomplish, and will speak frankly, confidentially, and honestly with me."

_____

_____

_____

_____

❖ Access Power From an Internal Mentor

A mentor can support you in navigating the political currents and "shoulds" of your organization. Ideally, the culture of the organization should not be political because many people don't want to engage with or judge the political environment. But it's important to be aware of politics and determine the best way to navigate your career growth given the climate. Begin by asking yourself the following questions:

➢ What will be my path to access some of that power?

➢ What relationships will be useful in carving out the type of career here that will give me the maximum ability to fulfill my talents?

➢ Who has positively impacted my career and personal growth thus far?

➤ Where can I expand my skills by utilizing my professional expertise to contribute to a project, nonprofit, or small business?

❖ **Start Designing Your Sponsors**

➤ Who can you count on to be committed to your success? / Who will you ask to be a part of your team that guides you towards that success?

➤ Who could be your sponsor or advocate within your organization, across your industry, and in the community?

> **KEANE INSIGHT**: One of the most rewarding aspects of being a leader is shaping an inspiring workplace culture. By building meaningful relationships, asking for help when needed, and fostering trust, you create a strong foundation for growth. Leveraging mentors and sponsors is essential to guide both your own development and that of your team, ensuring everyone thrives together.

Emerging leaders continued to come to me for career advice well after I left the corporate world. I got to know and like them and their work, particularly when they volunteered for an initiative I was leading, and we still meet periodically to stay connected. As they continue traveling along their career journeys, I get to celebrate their wins with them. Several of them have moved on to higher positions within the company and are successfully navigating new spaces. It's very exciting to share some tips and tricks for networking and designing the landscape. Through these experiences and similar ones, I've discovered that I'm a connector, bringing people together for win–win solutions. You never know where checking in on someone may lead. Assuming positive intent goes a long way, and we are stronger together.

If you want to get to the next level, if you want to get somewhere different, somewhere you aren't right now, you're going to have to be willing to try something new. And to try something new, you're going to have to take a risk. Take a deep breath and leap.

Team Engagement Video Series

A series of weekly videos offering practical strategies and activities to strengthen collaboration, foster connections, and build team resilience in the workplace. Each two-three minute video serves as an engaging meeting starter, combining light humor, actionable insights, and thought provoking discussion questions to inspire meaningful conversations and team cohesion.

CHAPTER 6

DELIVERING ON YOUR GOALS

Why did the scarecrow win an award?
He was outstanding in his field.

~John Brueckner, *World's Greatest Dad Jokes*

O nce you know your authentic self and understand your work environment (the landscape in which you operate) you're in a place where you can take action and deliver on your goals. You're no longer on the hamster wheel, and you have a feeling of control over yourself and your emotions and a sense of calm and confidence in the face of change. You see a clear path forward and can take steps within the vision of your organization that are also aligned with your personal goals. And when everything is in alignment, you begin to have even more of a sense of control over your destiny and your outward circumstances rather than always trying to navigate what life gives you (or throws at you).

Have you ever heard the expression, "Leap and the net will appear"? It's the idea that life rises up to meet us. The beautiful thing about this is that once we learn to navigate our landscape, we find that our landscape starts to transform into what we envisioned; it begins to come into alignment with who we are as individuals. You are a part of creating the life you want.

In essence, this state of alignment really is resilience in action. You've done the internal work of identifying what's most important to you, and you've designed the system to work around you. Now you're going after it.

Of course, you'll still get the occasional surprise, challenge, and setback at work and in your personal life. But when you're really delivering and engaging with the world from this powerful state, challenges start to seem less like overwhelming stressful events and more like opportunities to level up. Let's start by assessing where you are.

INVESTIGATION

Before we dive deeper, take a few minutes to jot down your responses to the following prompts:

1. What are your top three personal or professional goals?
2. What is currently your number one stressor, and how do you typically cope with it?
3. What activities bring you the most joy and fulfillment?

Now that you've written down your answers, consider how these elements align with your values and the vision you have for your life. Now, ask yourself these questions:

- When you think about your personal brand, how do you embody and achieve it?

- What are some of your secrets to taking action and delivering on your goals?

- What's holding you back from building stronger relationships at work or enhancing your personal brand?

- What steps can you take today to start aligning your actions with your goals?

By taking incremental, predetermined steps, you can deliver on your goals and create the life you envision for yourself. This journey starts with determining where you stand and what you need to shift to move closer to the life you want to live.

NAVIGATING CHANGE

Navigating change is an inevitable part of any journey towards achieving our goals. It's not just the destination but how we manage the twists and turns along the way that defines our resilience and success. To truly deliver on our goals, it's crucial to break down larger ambitions into specific, clear, and executable tasks. We must be able to take ownership of these tasks and hold ourselves accountable by monitoring our progress at every step. By doing so, we can see the small victories that propel us forward and recognize when adjustments are needed to keep moving in the right direction.

As you navigate change, ask yourself whether your goal is offering something unique or inventive that excites and challenges you. Does it ignite your creativity and push you to think outside the box? A goal that stretches our skills and aligns with our strategic vision will drive transformational change and open doors to new opportunities. However, following through on our goals isn't about adopting a pass-or-fail mentality. It's about staying flexible and allowing our journey to evolve. Life often presents unexpected detours, so the "why" behind our goals might shift or the goal itself might change. Embracing this flexibility saves us stress and enables us to realign our goals as needed, ensuring they continue to serve our broader vision.

Adapting to fluctuating demands is key when navigating change. The demands on our time and attention can shift rapidly, sometimes in ways we can't anticipate. You may have a well-planned schedule that includes time for joy and self-care, only to have it upended by unforeseen events. Psychological flexibility—your ability to stay in the present moment and adapt to these changes—will help you maintain balance and keep stress at bay. Reacting emotionally to disruptions can cloud your judgment, whereas staying focused on what can be done to adapt without compromising your values will keep you on course.

Shifting our perspectives is another vital component of navigating change. Being able to see a situation from different viewpoints, challenging our own assumptions, and being open to feedback fosters growth. In a team setting, this openness to diverse perspectives creates a collaborative environment where everyone feels valued, which in turn leads to more effective and inclusive decision-making. My own experiences with mentors taught me the importance of guiding others to shift their mindset and step beyond their comfort zones when navigating change. Now, as a mentor myself, I pay it forward by helping others develop the resilience to not just cope with what life throws at them but actively shape their own destinies. When everything is in alignment—your goals, values, and actions—you gain a greater sense of control over your circumstances and can turn challenges into opportunities for growth.

SETTING GOALS THAT ALIGN YOUR VISION AND ACTIONS

Aligning our vision with our actions is crucial for achieving meaningful and sustained success. When our actions are in harmony with our vision, we move forward with clarity and purpose, making decisions that are consistent with our long-term goals. This alignment ensures that every step we take is intentional, driving us closer to the life we envision for ourselves. It also provides a sense of fulfillment and motivation because we know that our daily efforts are contributing to something larger and more significant. Without this alignment, we risk wasting time and energy on tasks that don't serve our ultimate objectives, which can lead to frustration and a sense of being lost.

Setting such goals might feel daunting and time-consuming, but it takes only three main steps in the right direction:

1. IDENTIFY YOUR GOALS

To effectively deliver on your goals, it's essential to approach them with a combination of purpose, precision, and passion. This involves not only understanding why your goals matter to you but also taking deliberate, well-planned actions that are aligned with your vision.

Begin by identifying your goals, ensuring they resonate with your values and aspirations. Your goals should ignite your creativity and challenge you to grow, making the pursuit of them both exciting and rewarding. Here are some ways to do this:

- Determine what's most important to you and what brings you fulfillment.

- Imagine your ideal life in 5, 10, or 20 years, and identify the key elements that define success for you.

- Identify gaps between where you are and where you want to be, which represent areas for growth.

- Identify what you're good at and enjoy, then align these with your goals.

- Break down your vision into specific, actionable goals that align with your long-term impact, and review them regularly.

2. DESIGN A SMARTER VERSION OF YOUR GOALS BY USING KEANEST ELEMENTS™:

Once you've identified your goals, the next step is to design a smarter version of each one by incorporating "KEANEST" elements: Key, Effective, Actionable, Novel, Expected Date, Stimulating, and Timely. This process involves refining your goals into clear, actionable steps that are aligned with your broader vision. By doing so, you create a roadmap that both guides you and keeps you accountable, ensuring that each action you take is a meaningful step towards your desired outcome.

- ✓ **Key**: Make sure the identified goal is clear, precise, concise, and focused; in other words, a goal that's without a lot of noise. This prevents you from wasting your time and energy chasing squirrels or shiny new objects.

- ✓ **Effective**: To be effective, a goal needs to drive meaningful progress and measurable success, and it should be in line with your overall personal and professional vision and mission. This alignment ensures that the efforts you make contribute directly to your short-term and long-term objectives.

✓ **Actionable**: Whatever steps you decide to take towards the goal, they need to be translated into executable tasks that are specific and clear. You must be able to take ownership of these actionable tasks and hold yourself accountable by monitoring your progress along the way.

✓ **Novelty**: The goal needs to be an innovative one that differentiates you and ignites your growth. The best goals are ones that excite you; they ignite your creativity, challenge convention, and spark out-of-the-box thinking. When a goal is unique, it gives you a competitive advantage, opens the door to new opportunities, stretches your learning, enhances your skills, and aligns with your strategic vision, all of which drives transformational change.

✓ **Expected Date**: For any goal, it's a good idea to have a time stamp for when you would like to complete it. I like the term "expected" because it motivates you to move forward while also allowing for flexibility as you do so.

✓ **Stimulating**: A goal is best when it evokes a strong desire to achieve it, challenges the status quo, and drives your personal and professional growth. When a goal is stimulating to you, you feel inspired, enthusiastic, and committed to achieving it. It all starts with a vision, and that vision becomes success through passion.

✓ **Timely**: A goal must be within a specific timeframe that's strategically relevant to your current work and life conditions. It needs to be realistic and aligned with your broader business, market, and personal capacities, and it must help ensure that you have effective resources and a clear roadmap to achieve strategic success.

3. FOLLOW UP ON THAT GOAL

Finally, it is crucial to regularly follow up on your goals. Monitoring your progress helps you stay on track and allows for adjustments when necessary. Remember that your goals are not set in stone; life is dynamic, and your path may evolve as you discover new insights or face unexpected challenges. Regularly reassessing your goals ensures that they remain relevant and aligned with your vision, which helps you maintain momentum and achieve lasting success.

Here are some suggestions on how you can follow up on your goals:

- Monitor your progress using tools such as journals, checklists, or project management apps to ensure you stay on track.
- Set aside time periodically to review your goals, reflect on what's working, and identify areas that need adjustment.
- Be flexible and open to changing your goals or strategies based on new insights or unexpected challenges.
- Share your goals with a mentor, coach, or trusted peer to help keep you accountable and provide support.
- Acknowledge and celebrate small victories along the way to stay motivated and maintain momentum.

TAKING ACTION

Taking action with confidence and internal resilience doesn't just transform you as an individual; it also has a profound impact on those around you, particularly if you're in a leadership role.

When you step into the role of the leader of your own life, you model behaviors that inspire and motivate your team. Your confidence in your ability to achieve your goals translates into a more decisive and purposeful leadership style, which fosters a culture of resilience and determination within your team. When your team sees you confidently navigating challenges and consistently taking action towards your goals, they're more likely to adopt a similar mindset and approach their own tasks with greater commitment and drive.

Internal resilience, bolstered by confidence, also enables you to support your team more effectively during times of stress or uncertainty. As a leader, your ability to manage your own stress through spiritual, intellectual, emotional, and physical strategies equips you to guide your team through difficult situations with calm and clarity. Your resilience becomes a stabilizing force that helps maintain focus and morale within the group. Additionally, by demonstrating self-reliance and determination, you empower your team members to take ownership of their roles, encouraging them to take initiative and act with confidence in their own abilities.

Ultimately, the confidence and resilience you cultivate as a leader ripple outward, creating a positive, proactive environment in which your team feels supported, inspired, and capable of achieving their goals. Your leadership becomes not just about guiding others, but about fostering a collective sense of purpose and resilience that drives everyone towards shared success.

EXPLORATION

Now that you have more understanding of how you can deliver on your goals and how doing so impacts you and your team, let's reevaluate where you are and get you Going.

❖ **Identify Your Challenges and Successes**

This activity is designed to help you reflect on your recent experiences so you can both recognize the challenges you've faced and celebrate your successes. By doing so, you can better understand your strengths and recognize areas for improvement, as well as how to leverage your experiences for future growth, which ultimately brings clarity to your challenges and successes.

Apply these insights to identify your challenges and successes so that you can build future resilience:

1. Find a quiet space where you can focus without distractions. Take a few deep breaths to clear your mind.

2. Identify and write down three significant challenges you've recently faced. Be specific about what made them difficult.

3. Note how you addressed each challenge. What worked? What could have been better?

4. List three successes you had during the same period, no matter the size. Connect them to the challenges where possible.

5. Write down the key lessons you learned from both your challenges and successes. How can you apply these lessons going forward?

6. Share your reflections with a partner or a group so you can support each other in future challenges.

❖ **Identify Opportunities to Adjust**

This activity is designed to help you reflect on your current goals and strategies, continue identifying areas where adjustments may be needed, and start planning how to implement these changes for improved outcomes. In doing so, you'll gain a clear understanding of where and how to adjust your current strategies, which will lead you to more effective and efficient progress towards your goals.

1. Take a few minutes to list your current top goals, both personal and professional.

2. Evaluate your progress so far for each goal. Are you on track? Have you encountered any obstacles? If so, what have they been?

3. Identify areas where your approach may need adjustments, such as ineffective strategies, resource gaps, or the need for a different plan, and list at least two specific areas for improvement.

4. Brainstorm potential solutions or changes you could make for each identified area. Focus on actionable steps that align with your overall vision.

5. Prioritize the adjustments based on impact and feasibility. Which changes will bring you closer to your goals most effectively?

6. Develop a simple action plan for implementing these adjustments. Set a timeline and define the steps you need to take.

7. Monitor the results after implementing your adjustments. Reflect on how these changes impact your progress and make further tweaks as necessary.

❖ **Be a Go-Giver: The Five Laws of Stratospheric Success**

Success in business and life is not solely a result of ambition and hard work but also of the values and principles that guide our actions. The Five Laws of Stratospheric Success exemplify a philosophy that prioritizes giving, service, and authenticity, laying the groundwork for sustainable success. Each of these laws offers a pathway to creating meaningful and lasting impact both personally and professionally.

1. Value

   Our worth is measured not by our incomes but by the value we provide others. I didn't fully grasp this until entrepreneurs I mentored shared how my introductions of them to corporate leaders opened doors to their careers. Their gratitude reinforced the importance of the value I provided, which built trust and strong, lasting relationships. Consistently deliver exceptional value and you'll establish trust and build strong, enduring relationships.

2. Compensation

   Our income reflects the number of people we serve and how well we serve them. As my connections began to support me and provide opportunities that were invaluable in building my business, I began to realize that my network was my net worth. This experience taught me that compensation is more than financial; it's also about the service and support we give and receive. Focus on expanding your reach and enhancing the quality of your service to drive greater financial rewards.

3. Influence
   By prioritizing the interests of others, we cultivate influence and trust. I thrive on creating win–win situations in which mutual support leads to shared victories. This mindset has allowed me to build strong, influential relationships that benefit everyone involved. When people know you genuinely care about their needs, they're more likely to support you and advocate for your success.

4. Authenticity
   Your true self is your greatest asset. I strive to be the same person in every aspect of my life, whether at work, home, or in my spirituality. Not too long ago, a friend I hadn't seen in years told me that I was still the same bubbly, laughter-filled Nicole he had always known, which reminded me that authenticity fosters genuine, enduring connections. By being authentic, you connect with others on a deeper level, fostering genuine relationships that stand the test of time.

5. Receptivity
   Giving is important, but so is staying open to receiving. I used to struggle with accepting gifts, but I've learned that allowing others to give back is part of the reciprocal nature of success. Watching my husband and daughter light up with sheer

joy when I express how great their food is, for example, has shown me that receiving can bring just as much joy as giving, and sometimes more. Embrace the opportunities and support that come your way while recognizing that success is a reciprocal process in which giving and receiving are equally vital.

❖ **Measuring Joy's Impact**
How do you measure the impact of joy on workplace productivity?

- Through employee satisfaction surveys
- By observing team morale and engagement
- Tracking productivity and performance metrics

This question and your answers reflect your growing recognition of joy as a critical factor in workplace productivity and effectiveness. Maybe you think there *is* no way to measure the impact of joy. Yet, whether through employee satisfaction surveys, observations of team morale, or performance metrics, understanding how to measure the impact of joy in the workplace is essential for leaders aiming to create a thriving work environment. Each of the three listed methods offers a unique lens through which to view the benefits of fostering joy and highlights the diverse ways it can manifest into improved outcomes.

Poll results of our LinkedIn survey revealed that a significant majority of us believe fostering team morale and employee engagement are highly effective ways of measuring the impact of joy. This suggests that the relational and emotional aspects of work are highly valued and potentially more influential than traditional productivity metrics. However, the debate on whether joy's impact can be fully quantified continues, reflecting the complexity of this intangible yet powerful element in the workplace.

While joy's influence on the workplace is widely acknowledged, research indicates that fully capturing its impact requires a blend of quantitative and qualitative approaches.[47] Recognizing the limitations of conventional metrics, organizations might benefit from adopting more holistic evaluation methods that account for both the tangible and intangible benefits of fostering joy at work. Engaging in this conversation helps you understand how joy affects your well-being as an individual as well as your organizational success, which in turn empowers leaders to make informed decisions that enhance both employee satisfaction and business outcomes.

KEANE INSIGHTS. **KEANE INSIGHT**: Aligning your goals with your vision and taking consistent action are keys to success. I recommend using a "Joy Check": Regularly assess your progress, challenges, and successes while staying flexible as you navigate change. It's important to find innovative ways to help people be their best selves. Measuring joy in the workplace serves as a strong indicator of a thriving culture. By reflecting on your actions and making adjustments as needed, you can create an environment where everyone thrives with purpose and fulfillment.

As leaders, when we align our actions with our authentic selves and the vision of our organizations, we create the foundation for meaningful and sustained success. By applying the KEAN-EST elements, staying flexible, and embracing resilience, you can turn challenges into opportunities for growth, both for yourself and for your team. The Five Laws of Stratospheric Success remind us that success is not just about hard work but about the value we provide, the relationships we build, and the ability to give and receive openly. By fostering this mindset, you create a joyful, thriving environment that drives both personal fulfillment and organizational success.

Mastermind Group Coaching

An exclusive virtual network for leaders to share insights, overcome challenges, and develop resilience strategies. Facilitated by expert coaches, this group builds connection support, and best practices for leadership in hybrid work settings.

PART 3

THE ENDEAVOR

Are you busy playing out the life others have designed for you? This is your opportunity to apply what you've learned to get Ready by discovering yourself, get Set by designing your own landscape, and get Going to deliver on your goals.

First, take a moment to breathe. Close your eyes and take three deep, slow breaths.

Now ask yourself, "What do I want? Where do I want to go? Not what's in front of me, but what do I see ahead of me? Five years ahead of me? Ten years ahead of me?" It's okay to think about what you want and whether you're in alignment with that path.

I started by rediscovering myself, which meant I had to dive deep to discover my joy and shift my mindset. I then had to redesign my landscape and determine who I needed to connect with to grow. Finally, I had to deliver on my goals. My own experiences and those with my mentors along my career journey equipped me to give back to others. Now I want to pay it forward by mentoring you, helping you find opportunities, and guiding you towards action so that you're equipped with the resilience that allows you to successfully navigate change with a new mindset—and some joy.

Get ready and get set, because you're about to take action.

CHAPTER 7

READY

Did you hear about the new automatic shovel?
It's a groundbreaking invention.

~John Brueckner, *World's Greatest Dad Jokes*

As you embark on your journey of resilience, the first and perhaps most crucial step is self-discovery. Understanding who you are and what brings you joy is foundational to building resilience. This process is about more than just identifying what you enjoy; it's about recognizing the activities that help you navigate stress and challenges. Taking the time to explore your preferences and passions is key to developing a resilient mindset, as it grounds you in what truly matters and gives you the strength to face adversity with confidence.

Discovering yourself also involves more than finding surface-level enjoyment; it involves becoming aware of the experiences that make you feel most alive and at peace. Whether it's music, cycling, cooking, or any other activity that

enthralls you, these moments are more than just hobbies—
they are your anchors. They are the spaces where you can
retreat, recharge, and prepare yourself mentally for the challenges ahead. This is the place where you get to reflect on the
activities that not only bring you joy but also transport you
to a different mindset, one in which stress fades and you feel
empowered and centered.

In working through this first step of the resilience model
myself, I found that I enjoy five things the most: dancing, gardening, reading, drinking a nice cup of hot tea, and golfing, my
newest found passion. These are the things I gravitate towards
when stressed or preparing for a challenge. Take a moment to
think about what you like to do and how you're in a completely
different headspace when immersed in that activity.

I cannot stress this point enough: Understanding and
engaging in the activities that bring you joy and peace is not
just a way to unwind, it's a powerful tool for building resilience. By getting ready—both mentally and emotionally—
you set the stage for success in any challenge you face. This
preparation allows you to approach obstacles with a clear
mind, rooted in the strength and calm that comes from knowing yourself deeply. It's in these moments of readiness that
resilience is cultivated, resilience that enables you to bounce
back stronger and achieve your goals with greater confidence
and clarity.

HOW GETTING READY ENHANCES OUR RESILIENCE AND SUCCESS

Resilience is the cornerstone of professional success because
it allows us to navigate challenges and adapt to changes and
emerge stronger. It's not just about bouncing back from adversity but about growing through it, using setbacks as stepping

stones to greater achievements. Research shows that resilient professionals are more likely to view challenges as opportunities, a mindset that directly contributes to their long-term success.

Elizabeth Davis experienced a period of low resilience early in her career. While in college, she faced the traumatic experience of her father suffering a grand mal seizure that left him paralyzed. Balancing the emotional toll with her academic and social responsibilities could have easily overwhelmed her, led to decreased performance, and stalled her progress. However, Davis chose to compartmentalize her struggles, focusing on what she could control and gradually building the resilience necessary to overcome this challenge.

In contrast, Jeff Hoffman experienced high resilience repeatedly throughout his career. Despite facing numerous setbacks in his entrepreneurial journey, Hoffman consistently used these challenges as opportunities for growth. He pivoted when necessary and applied the lessons learned to fuel his future successes. His resilience helped him build a thriving business and established him as a successful and adaptable leader.

Just as with Davis and Hoffman, your resilience level can fluctuate at any time depending on your goals. For example, if your goal is a big career change, you might find that you need to tap into deeper reserves of strength and flexibility. On the other hand, when life is more stable and less demanding, you might not need to rely on your resilience as much. This adaptability shows that resilience isn't something you always use at the same level because it adjusts based on your current goals and the challenges you're facing. This dynamic nature of resilience is supported by research that highlights how resilience is not a fixed trait but a process that adapts according to the challenges at hand. For instance, a study on leadership and resilience during the COVID-19 pandemic found that leaders' resilience was activated differently depending on the specific goals they needed to achieve, such as maintaining healthcare services during a crisis.[48] This demonstrates how resilience can be mobilized in response to varying objectives and circumstances.

Recognizing that your resilience can fluctuate with your goals is key to navigating challenges effectively. As your circumstances change, your resilience needs may shift, requiring you to adapt and refocus your strengths. Let's start by discovering your strengths and assessing your level of resilience. Then we'll define who you are as a leader and explore how you can thrive in an uncertain and ever-changing world.

GET READY TO DISCOVER YOURSELF

Though in the pages of this book I can't sit with you and talk about your personal stressors or dive into problem-solving with you, what I can do is give you tools to help you grow and strengthen your resilience muscles. The key is to start by identifying your strengths, as that's what will really help you expand your ability to weather storms.

❖ DISCOVER YOUR STRENGTHS

Whether you realize it or not, your strengths are already a part of your brand. In chapter 4, you circled the words that represent your strengths and those that reflect your weaknesses. To prepare for designing your landscape, take some time to really think about those strengths and areas where you shine. If any new ones come to you, write them down. Keep them with you, as these strengths will be the foundation on which you later take action.

When I took this step of the resilience model, I discovered that the way others see me is not always the way I see myself. I also discovered that they could see things about me that I couldn't. For instance, during a speaking event, Hoffman introduced a branding exercise. I took the process seriously and immediately put it into action. I reached out to family members, colleagues, and even alumni groups, asking them to describe me in one word. This exercise revealed something profound: The way others see me isn't always how I see myself, and their feedback highlighted strengths I hadn't fully recognized. While I had been focusing on areas I thought were my strongest, others showed me that my real superpower was in areas I found effortless, such as building relationships and networking. This process not only helped me better understand my own strengths but also shifted my focus to areas where I could truly excel and stand out.

As I reflected on my educational background; my experiences in the corporate world and with thought leadership; and the insights I've gained through volunteering, being a member of a variety of organizations, and meeting people through speaking at conferences, I wrote down the things I saw as my strengths:

➢ Ambitious

➢ Empowering

➢ Fortifying

➢ Collaborative / Coalescing

➢ Systematic

> ➤ Compassionate / Uplifting
> ➤ Lighthearted / Joyful
> ➤ Adaptable
> ➤ Driven
> ➤ Connector

I also wrote down areas for improvement:

> ➤ Self-confidence
> ➤ Focus
> ➤ Evolving
> ➤ Goal-oriented

Then I asked my mentors how they saw me:

> ➤ Savvy / Resourceful
> ➤ Gracious
> ➤ Bridging
> ➤ Attuned
> ➤ Heart-leading / Harmonious
> ➤ Creative
> ➤ Reassuring
> ➤ Trustworthy
> ➤ Energizing

And I asked where they thought I could improve:

> ➤ Present-minded
> ➤ Content

➤ Purpose-driven / Inspired
➤ Storytelling
➤ Expansive

This experience was transformative. It helped me uncover who I truly am and align my professional efforts with my genuine strengths. By asking those who know me best, I gained invaluable clarity on my brand and discovered hidden assets that have propelled my career forward. This process also highlighted key areas for improvement, allowing me to take deliberate action to enhance my growth and effectiveness. Now I daily dedicate time to focus on being present-minded, regularly develop and share thought leadership content, and ensure my work is purpose-driven and aligned with my passions. And by integrating storytelling into my content and expanding my reach through national and international speaking associations, I've improved my skills and broadened my impact.

I encourage you to try this exercise yourself because focusing on what you're truly exceptional at and are passionate about while continually refining your strengths leads to greater fulfillment and success.

❖ DISCOVER YOUR RESILIENCE

What's Your Sphere of Resilience?™

Resilience can help you cope with stressful events and situations more easily. Building resilience means improving your ability to manage various aspects of your life more effectively. The questionnaire below represents the internal (spiritual, intellectual, emotional, physical) and external (social, professional, lifestyle, financial) factors that may affect your ability to manage stress.

Disclaimer: The scores on this assessment are not a substitute for a medical diagnosis or treatment. They are meant to help you identify areas in your life where you can improve resilience or reduce stress.

This assessment can help you evaluate your ability to manage elevated levels of stress and identify areas where you could improve resilience.

For each question, score yourself between 1 and 5, where

1 = Strongly Disagree, 2 = Disagree, 3 = Neutral, 4 = Agree, and 5 = Strongly Agree.

Internal Resilience	Resilience Type	My Score
1. I am clear on my purpose and my values no matter what happens.	Spiritual	
2. I have a strong sense of self.	Spiritual	
3. I can deal with whatever comes my way and focus on finding solutions when problems arise.	Intellectual	
4. I am working to attain specific goals and create my vision for the future.	Intellectual	
5. I try to see the funny side of things when something unexpectedly goes wrong, or I am dealing with an unpleasant situation.	Emotional	
6. Overall, I feel good emotionally and can overcome feelings of sadness, nervousness, and stress when they come up.	Emotional	
7. I am generally in good physical health and rarely get sick or experience one or more of the following: headaches, digestive problems, high blood pressure, concentration problems, muscle tension.	Physical	
8. I get 6 to 8 hours of sleep every night and feel alert during my work hours.	Physical	
Sub-Total: (Internal Resilience Score):		

KEANE
INSIGHTS.

External Resilience	Resilience Type	My Score
9. I have close and secure relationships with family members, friends, and my partner or spouse, and I spend time with others outside of my work hours.	Social	
10. I know where to turn for support and have positive working relationships with my colleagues.	Social	
11. Throughout my career, I have been able to successfully adapt to challenges and changes.	Professional	
12. I enjoy my work and have positive interactions with my colleagues or the people I work with.	Professional	
13. I have a healthy balance between my work and personal life and make time for my hobbies and personal interests.	Lifestyle	
14. My daily activities include time for the things I enjoy, such as hobbies and creative endeavors.	Lifestyle	
15. My finances are in good order; I know where the money is coming in and going out.	Financial	
16. If I were to lose my job today, I would have the resources to withstand the financial impact until something else came along.	Financial	
Sub-Total (External Resilience Score):		
TOTAL SCORE (Add Sub-Totals)		

RESULTS

If your **internal** resilience is **higher** than your external resilience:	You may find it challenging to reach out to others for help and might benefit from expanding your support system. Spending time with your spouse, children, or friends, having a hobby, or reaching out to a professional can help restore energy and provide a fresh perspective on problems.
If your **external** resilience is **higher** than your internal resilience:	Consider exploring activities that help develop emotional resilience or support your physical well-being. A good balance between external and internal resilience can help you create a more fulfilling life.

KEANE
INSIGHTS.

Write down the questions where you assigned lower scores.
These are the areas on which you can improve.

Based on your total score, check below to see which category fits you.

0—31	32—47	48—63	64—80
You have low resilience and high perceived or real stress. You may not feel in control of your workload or personal life, and you find it challenging to manage unexpected change. Consider developing your resilience by exploring your stress triggers and learning new skills that enhance resilience.	You may have difficulty managing stress or big changes in life or at work. You might have some coping strategies for dealing with challenging situations but could benefit from creating consistent healthy habits and tools to prevent and manage stress.	You have an average level of resilience. While there is room for improving your coping skills and resiliency in a few areas, you can manage setbacks or unexpected events in most areas of your life.	You have a high degree of resilience. Your score suggests that you have developed strong coping mechanisms that help you navigate stressful situations. You understand how to recognize, weather, or prevent stressful events or unexpected changes.

KEANE INSIGHT: Learn more about how you can develop your resilience and become effective at managing stress by reaching out to www.KeaneInsights.com.

❖ DISCOVER WHO YOU ARE AS A LEADER: STAND OUT FROM THE REST

Understanding and embracing your unique qualities as a leader is essential to setting yourself apart from others. This involves identifying your core values, strengths, and the attributes that make you uniquely suited to lead. When you gain a clear understanding of your leadership identity, you can make more intentional decisions, inspire those around you, and create a lasting impact within your organization.

It's important to recognize that many leaders are often unaware of their true strengths and areas that require growth. Research published in the *Journal of Business Ethics* reveals that leaders frequently overestimate their abilities and are unaware of how they are perceived by others, and this lack of self-awareness can hinder their effectiveness and prevent them from fully realizing their leadership potential.[49] To stand out as a leader, it is crucial to go beyond technical skills and strategic thinking. While these assets are important, what truly sets exceptional leaders apart is their ability to connect with others on a deeper level, engage their teams, and elevate those around them. This involves being authentic, effectively communicating their vision, and continuously developing themselves and their teams.

You can start making yourself stand out as a leader by reflecting on your past experiences, seeking feedback from those you trust, and aligning your leadership style with your personal values. By doing so, you not only clarify your leadership identity but position yourself as a leader who can inspire and drive meaningful change. This process of self-discovery and continuous improvement is key to standing out in your field and achieving long-term success on your leadership journey.

To effectively recognize and motivate employees, consider three key approaches:

1. Public Acknowledgment
   Highlight individual achievements during team meetings or company events, such as praising a team member for completing a challenging project on time.

2. Personalized Rewards
   Tailor recognition to the unique values of each employee, whether it's a formal award, bonus, time off, or professional development opportunities.

3. Peer Recognition Programs
   Encourage employees to acknowledge each other's contributions through initiatives such as peer-nominated awards or a "shout-out" board; these strategies boost morale and foster a collaborative and supportive team environment.

By consistently recognizing performance, you enhance not only individual satisfaction and engagement but also the overall team dynamic. When employees feel valued and appreciated, they're more likely to work together effectively, which leads to a stronger, more cohesive team and a positive organizational culture in which everyone is motivated to contribute their best.

Organizations are constantly linking their strategy to desired outcomes. Strategic imperatives are vital to company growth. If you're a leader, you already understand the importance of business, strategic, and financial acumens to meeting your organizational goals. You may also be aware of the greatness within you: your self-knowledge, your integrity, and your resilience from your years of experience in this ever-changing world. Yet what can differentiate you from the rest is the vital task of engaging the greatness of others. Why? To improve performance and add health to your organization and to help you stand out from the rest. It's a win–win for all! So, be contagious. Everyone is uplifted when you share your positive qualities with others and look for innovative ways to help people be their best selves.

❖ DISCOVER PERFORMANCE THROUGH RECOGNITION

The impact of peers supporting each other through difficult times is remarkable. Whether personally or publicly, when an employee or team member is recognized often—and especially when it unexpectedly comes from their leaders—their brain releases oxytocin. Neuroscience studies indicate that oxytocin affects an individual's willingness to accept social risks arising through interpersonal interactions. On the individual level, this type of connection results in 29% more satisfaction, 40% less burnout, 74% less stress, and 106% more energy. On the organizational level, it results in 13% fewer sick days, 50% higher productivity, 76% more employee engagement.[50]

Imagine my pleasant surprise when I was a part of a team where members were recognized for all their individual contributions—above and beyond their job duties—for the betterment of the department and ultimately the betterment of the organization. And this was done in a company-wide presentation given by the director, who now shares it on the department's internal website. The recognition was personal, public, and unexpected.

How will you constantly strive to enhance the relationship between you and your employees as well as build each one to collaborate effectively as a cohesive team? Along with fostering collaboration within your team, strengthening the connection between you and your employees requires a strategic focus on communication, trust building, and consistent recognition of their efforts. One of the most effective ways to achieve this is through performance recognition, which acknowledges individual contributions while also encouraging a more unified and productive team environment.

❖ DISCOVER YOUR TEAM

➤ Start your team meetings by asking these five questions:

1. How can we make our work more personalized, connected, and aligned with the organization's goals?

2. How do we ensure our service offerings support the whole health of individuals?

3. What steps can we take to streamline and simplify our processes?

4. How can we incorporate a forward and sustainable approach?

5. How can we enhance and impact our organization's overall culture?

➤ Engage your team by creating mission and vision statements.

Creating mission and vision statements with your team is a powerful way to align everyone with an organization's goals and values. A mission statement focuses on what your team is doing currently and confirms your value to the company, while a vision statement looks towards the future and outlines what your team aspires to achieve. By involving your team in crafting these statements, you ensure that everyone is committed to the shared goals and understands their roles in achieving them. For example, you might create a mission statement that defines how your team serves customers and a vision statement that describes the broader impact your team hopes to have on the organization and the industry. This collaborative process fosters a sense of ownership and inspires your team to work together towards a common purpose.

❖ DISCOVER YOUR ORGANIZATION

As a leader, one of the most crucial aspects of your role is to deeply understand and define the identity of your organization. This process begins with an alignment of your team's strategy and goals with the overarching company objectives. By facilitating discussions around mission, vision, and values, you can help your team see how their daily work contributes to the bigger picture.

To effectively align your team's efforts with broader organizational goals, start by asking critical questions during team meetings that link your employees' work to the company's strategy, such as exploring ways to enhance customer engagement through an innovative approach. This helps clarify how your team can make a meaningful impact. Next, focus on building a strong team identity by collaboratively developing a mission statement that defines what your team does, who they serve, and how they serve them. Complement this with a vision statement that aligns your team's aspirations with the company's future direction, ensuring everyone is working towards the same goals. Finally, create a cohesive team name that encapsulates your mission and vision, which solidifies your team's identity and fosters a sense of pride and belonging within the organization.

By guiding your team through these exercises, you not only discover more about your organization but also empower your team to see themselves as integral to its success. This process of discovery and alignment can lead to a more engaged, motivated, and effective team, driving better results for the whole organization.

TAKE INSIGHT INTO ACTION

The concept of taking insight into action is where resilience becomes the driving force behind your success. Resilient people don't just survive challenges, they thrive by taking purposeful steps that transform their insights into real, tangible outcomes. Ultimately, the journey of resilience is about taking well-planned actions, setting clear milestones, and tracking your progress. It's not just about knowing what to do but about having the courage and determination to follow through. As we embark on this journey together, remember that resilience isn't just about bouncing back but about moving forward with intention, confidence, and a plan for success.

While effective leadership is about managing tasks and deadlines, it's also about fostering an environment where creativity, productivity, and well-being thrive. To drive positive change and sustain long-term success, leaders must carve out time to strategize, set boundaries, and invest in personal and team development. Here are some ways you can do this:

➤ Block off time on your calendar to strategize. Strategy requires uninterrupted time to focus and allow space for creativity and productivity. Sometimes the moments that seem like you're not doing anything are the moments when you're actually laying the groundwork for everything you need to achieve.

➤ Set boundaries and manage your time by preserving your energy at home and in the workplace. The three most effective ways to do this are through setting routines, delegating, and fostering trust. By doing so, you ensure that your energy is spent on activities that make the most impact.

➤ Bring positive change to those who rely on you. There are many resources out there for improving yourself and your team, including executive coaches for one-on-one consultations as well as digital educational tools and apps. I've added some of them to the Reader Resources at the end of this book. You could also consider retreats that focus on mindfulness, stress relief, and personal growth; offer an immersive experience designed to rejuvenate and inspire; and provide new perspectives and strategies.

➤ Engage, connect with, and retain your team members through humor. Start meetings, presentations, and brainstorming sessions with a work-appropriate themed joke to lighten the mood, create an atmosphere of trust, and foster creativity. A simple laugh can set the tone for a more open and productive discussion.

➤ Take pauses to connect with your employees and connect one-on-one with your direct reports. This approach allows for deeper understanding, better communication, and stronger relationships. Even brief interactions can significantly boost morale and foster a sense of belonging.

➤ Steer your team towards a positive future by displaying quotes about positive leadership that are inspirational and motivating. Engage them in self-care and culture-of-inclusion exercises to strengthen the team's cohesion and commitment to shared goals.

➤ Participate in professional development opportunities. Continuing education is vital for growth. Whether it's attending workshops, enrolling in courses, or joining industry conferences, these opportunities help you stay current and bring fresh ideas back to your team. Examples include leadership seminars, online courses, and industry-specific conferences.

➤ Discover your Leadership Type via <u>BREAKTHRU Brands</u>. Visionary Laura Barnard founded BREAK-THRU and is dedicated to her mission of transforming the landscape of leadership. Understanding your Leadership Type is essential for effective management, and tools like this one can help you identify your strengths and areas for improvement, which will allow you to lead more authentically.

➤ Remember to prioritize your health and well-being. It's the backbone needed to meet any goal. Taking care of your physical and mental health means you ensure that you have the energy and resilience needed to meet your goals and support your team effectively.

KEANE INSIGHT: Make time for what's important. With all the changes happening with AI, it's important to remember that it's human connection that counts. Take time to ensure you're prioritizing yourself, which allows you to be present for your family, friends, team, organization, and community. I encourage you to reach out to three people you haven't connected with in the last three months and catch up with them. Call them, schedule a meal with them, or engage in a joyful activity together.

As you embark on the journey of discovering yourself, your resilience, and your strengths as a leader, remember that true leadership begins with self-awareness and a commitment to continuous growth. By recognizing your own potential and nurturing the talents of your team, you set the stage for transformative performance. Take these insights into action:

✓ Carve out time for strategic thinking.
✓ Establish boundaries that protect your energy.
✓ Embrace tools such as joyful retreats to rejuvenate and inspire.

These practices will not only enhance your leadership but also elevate the entire organization.

Immersive Retreat:

An intensive experience for leaders and teams to prevent burnout while enhancing leadership and building resilience. This retreat combines mindfulness, stress relief, and personal growth with practical leadership exercises and strategic preparation. Designed to rejuvenate and inspire, it offers tools and perspectives to navigate challenges with purpose and joy.

CHAPTER 8

SET

Did you hear about the clown who held doors for people?
It was a nice jester.

~John Brueckner, *World's Greatest Dad Jokes*

A s you begin to harness the power of self-awareness and strengthen your resilience as a leader, it's essential to move beyond introspection and into action. Leadership isn't just about understanding your own potential; it's about shaping an environment in which you and your team can flourish. Now, let's take that next step together. As we move forward, I will guide you through the process of designing the landscape for your leadership journey. We will explore how to create an environment that fosters innovation, inclusivity, and sustainable success, setting the foundation for your vision to thrive.

HOW GETTING SET ENHANCES OUR RESILIENCE AND SUCCESS

The Set stage of the resilience model is crucial for finding joy, reducing stress, and building resilience. Getting set involves preparing yourself mentally, emotionally, and spiritually for the challenges you'll face. You do that by ensuring you have the tools and mindset needed to effectively navigate life's ups and downs. When you're Set, you can approach situations with clarity, purpose, and a sense of control, which significantly reduces the stress you experience and enhances your ability to not only bounce back from adversity but propel forward in designing your future.

Liza Rossi's journey with the Ekukhanyeni Relief Project in South Africa illustrates the power of being Set. Early in her career, when she wasn't fully Set, Rossi experienced the negative effects of being stressed and feeling overwhelmed: "I burned out a few times where my physical body got ill." Facing immense challenges—financial constraints, social resistance, and the responsibility of caring for thousands of children—Rossi maintained her resilience and joy by getting Set internally. Through regular spiritual practices such as meditation and prayer, she kept herself centered, enabling her to approach each day with purpose and clarity. Once she aligned her internal world with her external actions, she regained her footing, strengthened her resilience, and found renewed joy in her mission. As she puts it, "When you are truly set within yourself, you can bring through the love and joy in what you do, and that cancels out the stress and anxiety."

Rossi's experience underscores the importance of being Set. By preparing yourself mentally, emotionally, and spiritually, you can better handle stress, maintain your joy, and build the resilience needed to thrive in all areas of life. Prioritizing this internal foundation allows you to navigate challenges with grace and purpose.

GET SET TO DESIGN YOUR LANDSCAPE

Remember when I said that to do something different, you're going to have to take a risk? That might be something you don't want to hear. Maybe you're struggling because you aren't getting to that next place or breaking through to the next test. But maybe that's because you're still playing it safe.

It's not easy to take risks. I fought that for a while myself, believing that I didn't need to change something because everything was working just fine. But years later, I was still getting the same results. I worked with one of my mentors to answer some thoughtful questions, and he said to me, "Nicole, do you realize based on all your answers here that you never take risks?" I took that as a challenge and said, "I take calculated risks." But I realized he was right. I sat with this for a while as I continued on in the corporate world for several more years (not taking risks), until one day when I took my first calculated risk by deciding to form the right relationships for me. And that's where I found the mentors who helped me find my joy and resilience—and my success.

Sometimes resilience involves having the bravery to take a risk when you know change is needed because the status quo just isn't working for you anymore. But you're the safest bet there is—take a risk on yourself. Together, we'll make the risk more manageable as I guide you through practical ways you can start designing the landscape of your life.

❖ DESIGN YOUR RELATIONSHIPS

Did you know you can build relationships 15 minutes at a time? When a company is going through a change, the first questions that come to mind are usually "Is there a place for me?" and "How do I navigate change to survive and thrive during this challenging time?" The answer is, through resiliency. And I achieved that by gaining mentors who've pushed me to self-reflect, take risks, and make critical choices.

One tool I used for networking and relationship building is the 15-Minute Calendar Strategy™. When I saw someone doing something I found interesting or who I wanted to learn from, I asked for 15 minutes on their calendar. As I met with each of them, I gained both mentors and sponsors. I shared with my mentors the amazing things I was doing and where I wanted to go, and I asked them for feedback on how to get there. The next thing I knew, opportunities were landing in my lap, whether three months, six months, or sometimes a year later.

Through building relationships, you gather beautiful colors of possibility with which to paint and place yourself in the position to be cared for personally and challenged directly. And the 15-Minute Calendar Strategy works throughout all levels of an organization. I once had a meeting with a C-suite executive during which I shared all the amazing work I'd done and the work I was currently leading. I was feeling really great about myself. Within five minutes, this mentor was able to see me and assess what I needed to do to get to the next level in my career journey.

Karélix Alicea's expert feedback on the 15-Minute Calendar Strategy highlights its practicality and effectiveness, particularly for entrepreneurs: "I definitely see the value in networking and in just 15 minutes; that way, you don't feel like you're asking for so much." Her journey involved building mentor relationships organically, and she emphasizes the importance of surrounding ourselves with individuals who offer strengths and insights that complement your own. Alicea's belief that "forming relationships and dealing with change is a given" aligns with the essence of the 15-Minute Calendar Strategy, demonstrating how brief, focused interactions can help entrepreneurs build a strong support system. This is essential for personal and professional growth as well as for fostering resilience in the face of change.

When implementing the 15-Minute Calendar Strategy, it's just as important to give our time in return. For every 15 minutes I received from someone, I made it a goal to do the same for someone else. This strategy is like keeping a checking account: If you take money out, then it's time to put a deposit back in. Always try to keep a balance. Maybe it's just karma that makes everything right and helps keep this world in a beautiful balance.

In addition to the 15-Minute Calendar Strategy, there are many other ways to build relationships as entrepreneurs and intrapreneurs.

1. Leverage organic connections.
   Rather than forcing connections at large events, use opportunities like conventions to introduce yourself and get to know others. Share contact information to nurture these relationships while also focusing on deepening connections with those whom you naturally resonate. Surround yourself with like-minded individuals and invest time in repeated interactions.

2. Be vulnerable and share your journey.
   People connect more deeply when you're open about your challenges and failures. When peers share their struggles, it fosters a stronger sense of connection because both parties realize that even successful entrepreneurs face the same challenges. This openness can

lead to meaningful relationships in which support and opportunities naturally arise.

3. Build comfort through consistency.

 Attend conferences and social events regularly to build familiarity and comfort with others. Over time, this can lead to genuine friendships and business relationships. Repeatedly attending the same events to build rapport helps reduce the discomfort often associated with networking.

4. Focus on small, purposeful interactions.

 Use the 15-Minute Calendar Strategy to build relationships gradually. Ask for short meetings to discuss mutual interests or get feedback. This approach is less overwhelming and can lead to long-term mentorships. Over time, brief focused meetings with potential mentors lead to significant career opportunities.

5. Integrate your personal life with your professional relationships.

 Many of us were taught to keep our personal and professional lives separate. The culture of large organizations often dictates that it's not appropriate to share personal matters; we're expected to appear strong at work and trust only our family and friends. However, in small businesses, integrating our personal life with trusted professional relationships can actually strengthen bonds and create a more supportive work environment.

6. Expand your resilience through connection.

 In challenging times, lean on your relationships for support. Whether through mentors, peers, or employees, these connections can provide the strength and encouragement needed to persevere. Rely on your support system, including your partner and employees, and maintain a level of transparency to foster trust as you navigate the difficulties of running a business, especially during a crisis.

When you enter into a mentor relationship, it's important to have boundaries. At Keane Insights, we make sure there's a tight boundary between our 15-minute mentorship moments and our coaching and consulting opportunities. Equally respect your own boundaries as a mentor and those of your mentors.

❖ DESIGN YOUR MENTORS

Embracing mentorship can be a powerful stepping stone in advancing your career. Tapping into your mentors' vast reservoir of experience, wisdom, and guidance unlocks your full potential. These relationships build your confidence and skills to overcome challenges and empower you to seize opportunities for professional development.

While it can be daunting to start connecting with mentors, the more you ask for help, the easier and less risky it feels, making it an invaluable step in the journey towards resilience. By investing in mentor–mentee relationships, you propel your career forward, nurture your leadership acumen, and successfully navigate the complexities of the modern workplace. Mentorship also fosters the emergence of effective leaders, serves as a guiding compass, and bridges the gap between newcomers and seasoned veterans. Mentors can also become powerful advocates and sponsors who help transform your career and take it to new heights.

To get started, it helps to approach the process with the right questions. Though they can vary according to time, place, person, and circumstance, here are six questions I've found to be the most effective when working to gain mentors:

1. What are some of your goals?
2. How do your goals align with my department?
3. What are some of the challenges?
4. What do you think would help align our goals and overcome these challenges?
5. How can we continue to partner for success and contribute to making a positive impact?
6. I would like to continue this conversation. What cadence would you recommend for touching base? Would every two months work for you?

❖ DESIGN YOUR NETWORK

I am known for my ability to network and build connections. I didn't realize the magnitude of this until I was asked to moderate a session called "Turning Connections into Business Opportunities" at a healthcare and life sciences conference. To expand my own sphere of influence, one of the best methods that works for me is conference networking. Attending conferences is a wonderful way to stay up to date on the latest trends in the market, learn about innovative advancements in your industry, and have conversations with like-minded peers.

Expanding your sphere of influence at a conference goes well beyond attending the breakout sessions. The magic is in the insights gained, the relationships ignited, and the future partnerships built. When you master the art of networking at this macro level, you have the essential strategies and tools needed to successfully prepare for and navigate industry conferences.

Like any kind of networking, conference networking doesn't need to be complicated. It's simply about connecting directly with the people around you. Here are some of the questions I often ask others seated next to me:

➤ How are you enjoying the conference?

➤ Which session has been the most impactful?

➤ What did you think of the last speaker?

➤ I have a follow-up question for you, if you don't mind . . . May I have your contact information? I would like to keep in touch. Here's mine.

After a conference, I like to follow up with the contacts I made within 48 hours. Sometimes I'll stay an extra day at the hotel to conduct all my post-conference tasks. There are many topics of potential discussion for your connections, including what you learned from the conference speakers and the overall content. It's also helpful to give information during your follow-up. You can share two takeaways from the conference or other conferences you've attended that cover similar topics.

Here are some of the steps to help you design your landscape through conference networking:

➤ Preconference Preparation:

✓ Optimize your marketing materials and digital presence. Make sure you have all your materials (e.g., business cards, brochures, etc.) and that your website and social media profiles are up to date.

✓ Effectively research the attending companies and attendees and identify how they align with your career and business goals.

✓ Set clear and measurable objectives for the conference. Ask yourself, "By the end of this conference, three takeaways are . . ." (e.g., number of leads, partnerships to forge, etc.)

✓ Craft compelling elevator pitches to share your unique value with confidence and clarity at the right time. This is where emotional intelligence comes into play.

➤ During the Conference
Make meaningful connections by engaging with both visitors and fellow attendees. This includes actively listening for potential business opportunities. While attending sessions, raise your visibility through participation and asking thought-provoking questions. I remember attending a conference breakout session, and a peer whispered a wonderful question to me. I recommended that she ask that question to the panelists. Guess what? My peer was asked to come sit on the next conference panel! Her question was so thought-provoking that it shed light on her sphere of expertise.

➤ Post-Conference Analysis and Relationship Building

✓ Immediately follow up with your contacts. There is great significance in having timely follow-up conversations to reinforce the connections you made at a conference. This can be done using a customer relationship management tool to track leads and interactions made during the conference. It's a perfect example of how the innovations in AI can be used to foster relationships between human beings rather than replace them.

✓ Analyzing success and areas for improvement involves reviewing your initial objectives to assess the conference outcomes against your predefined goals. Take time to gather feedback from your new contacts and team to help you refine future approaches. Like athletes after a game, review your objectives like a game tape with your coach and teammates, assess the strengths and areas for improvement, then get back out there and play the next game.

✓ Build long-term relationships by designing and implementing strategies to maintain and grow relationships with the contacts you made during the conference. Through these relationships, you can leverage your learning and enhance your long-term business strategy.

Additional Notes:

- If you're conducting a virtual conference session, use interactive elements such as polls and Q&A sessions to engage the audience.

- Distribute resources by providing attendees with a digital resource pack that includes a checklist for conference preparation, templates for follow-up emails, and a list of further reading materials.

- Cover all technical requirements and ensure all participants have access to the necessary technology. Provide technical support contacts for any issues during the training.

❖ DESIGN YOUR EMPLOYEES

Zig Ziglar famously said, "You don't build a business. You build people, and people build the business."[51] And Kevin Cope, the founder of Acumen Learning, notes that there are five key drivers of any business, and without the fifth, the other four (cash, profit, assets, and growth) cease to exist. What is that fifth driver that powers our business? People! It's good employees who make wise decisions and provide value to our paying customers. As leaders, we can design our employees to drive the business.

As we've already seen, engagement and productivity are linked. Yet a striking 70% of employees are disengaged.[52] When employees have a disengaged mindset, they put in only enough effort to get their paychecks and not get fired; they aren't giving their talent, energy, or passion. This means organizations aren't tapping into bright ideas that could lead to creativity and innovation.

Leaders hold the key to shaping the success of themselves and their employees by intentionally designing strategies that foster engagement, inclusion, and alignment with the organization's mission. In a workplace where employees often dread coming to work, feel unsafe voicing their opinions, and/or struggle with feeling respected or valued, it is crucial for leaders to take proactive steps to develop their teams. By offering feedback, coaching, and support, leaders can create a psychologically safe environment that promotes high job satisfaction and reduces turnover.

How do we as leaders tap into this creativity and innovation? How do we engage people at work in ways that drive better results in our organizations? The answer is right at our fingertips: connection. Jeff Hoffman emphasizes the power of connection and transparent leadership in building a thriving workforce that drives business success. He highlights the importance of creating a supportive environment where employees feel safe to take risks, learn from failures, and grow together. Reinforcing the value of collaboration and continuous learning, Hoffman advises leaders, "Focus on what you're truly good at and don't be afraid to ask for help." By fostering trust, encouraging open communication, and building a strong support network, leaders can empower their employees to contribute meaningfully to the organization's long-term success.

To build a strong foundation for a thriving workplace that drives long-term business success, leaders must focus on key strategies that develop and empower connections among their employees. Here are five essential tips for doing this:

1. Foster open communication and encourage regular feedback and open dialogue to ensure employees feel heard and valued.

2. Promote continuous learning by investing in ongoing professional development to help employees grow and contribute more effectively.

3. Recognize and reward efforts frequently through acknowledgment of employee achievements to boost morale and engagement.

4. Create a psychologically safe environment and build a culture where employees can take risks and express themselves without fear of judgment.

5. Encourage autonomy and ownership, which empowers employees by giving them control over their work and decision-making processes, in turn fostering innovation and accountability.

❖ DESIGN YOUR LEADERSHIP BRAND

Remember the strengths you discovered about yourself when you were getting ready? Now's the time to put those strengths into action by designing them as your brand attributes. If you don't already have a brand statement, or if your current one isn't capturing what your business is really about or representing your professionally authentic self, here's your opportunity to design the landscape of your brand.

Designing your brand statement is about championing resiliency through determining your brand goals, specifying your brand values, and positioning your brand for greater impact. It's about shifting from a limited mindset to a limitless mindset. For instance, when I was designing my personal brand, I made a list of my former leadership titles:

- Supplier Development Leader
- Healthcare Senior Manager
- Public Speaker
- Licensed Family Therapist
- Board Member

Upon reflection, I realized I needed to reframe my experiences with a limitless mindset:

- Strategic Healthcare Executive
- Procurement and Supplier Expert
- Champion of Movement & Mindset
- Inspirational Speaker & Connector
- Licensed Mental Health Therapist
- Active Board Member, Advisor & Mentor

When I embarked on the journey of defining my business's brand, I knew that the foundation had to be built on a clear purpose, mission, and vision. Our brand at Keane Insights is not just about what we do but why we do it. At its core, our purpose is to champion resiliency and enhance the lives of others. Each day, our mission drives us to guide others in discovering joy by helping them overcome challenges through agility, meaningful connections, access to resources, and a deeper spiritual understanding of their essence. This mission aligns with my personal vision of a future where people are united through harmony and love and empowered to live authentically and purposefully.

To effectively communicate this, it was essential for me to shift from a limited mindset focused on titles to a limitless mindset that reflects the true essence of my leadership and expertise. For example, while titles like "Behavioral Health Clinical Manager," "Licensed Marriage and Family Therapist," and "Healthcare Senior Manager" are accurate, they don't fully capture the impact of my work. By reframing these experiences, I can better articulate my roles as a "Strategic Healthcare Executive" and "Mental Health Expert," which resonate more deeply with our brand's values and goals. By reframing my professional titles from specific roles to broader identities, I can better communicate the impact and leadership I and my business bring to the healthcare field.

This shift highlights my commitment to fostering resilience; promoting mental wellness; creating inclusive, supportive work environments; and aligning our brand with our broader mission to drive meaningful change in healthcare. This reframing allowed me to position our brand as one that empowers others to find resilience and joy, navigate challenges, and promote spiritual harmony and inclusivity.

To activate this brand positioning effectively, I identified key audiences and channels that align with my and my business's expertise and message. Healthcare and behavioral health professionals, corporate leadership and HR executives, and community organizations are at the forefront of our outreach. By leveraging professional conferences, corporate training programs, webinars, and publications, we can share our insights on leadership, team resilience, and organizational culture, furthering our mission of empowering resilience and fostering inclusive, supportive cultures.

As a leader, I embrace the role of being a connector: someone who builds relationships, fosters trust, and creates outcomes greater than the sum of their parts. This leadership style is deeply influenced by altruism and enjoyment, both of which guide my thoughts and actions in uniting others through building communities, forming networks, crafting partnerships, and forging bonds. My business's brand positioning reflects this by emphasizing the importance of helping others create meaningful connections and promoting a culture of inclusiveness and resilience in both personal and professional settings.

In every communication, my tone remains active, committed, and nurturing, ensuring that our message resonates with authenticity and warmth. Whether through empowering resilience from insight to action or harmonizing the essence of self and society, our goal at Keane Insights is to lead organizations and individuals towards a resilient future where agility, connection, and spiritual mindfulness are the cornerstones of success.

By leveraging your expertise, you can clearly define and communicate your brand in a way that embodies your purpose, mission, and vision. You can demonstrate a limitless mindset as a lifelong learner and design an inclusive culture that fosters growth and elevates your leadership.

❖ DESIGN AN INCLUSIVE CULTURE

Designing your landscape involves intentionally shaping the environment in which you operate, both personally and professionally, to foster growth, resilience, and success, but it's much more than that. It's also about continuously developing your own skills and connections to navigate the evolving culture of your workplace. It involves creating a workplace culture that both supports and celebrates the diverse strengths and perspectives of each generation, from the wisdom of the silent generation and baby boomers to the balance and experience of Gen X-ers and the innovation of millennials and Gen Z-ers.

In our presentation called "Harmonious Leaders," I emphasize the importance of recognizing and harnessing these generational strengths. By doing so, leaders can create a culture of inclusivity where all employees feel valued and motivated. This approach not only enhances team performance but also builds a resilient organization capable of navigating the complexities of today's dynamic workplace.

In his book *Culture by Design*, David J. Friedman reinforces this concept by advocating for a deliberate approach to shaping organizational culture. He emphasizes that culture is not a byproduct of circumstance but a strategic asset that when designed with intention can drive long-term success.[53] By setting the stage for a culture that is both inclusive and resilient, leaders can ensure their teams are well-equipped to thrive amid change and adversity.

By engaging in ongoing learning and building a strong support network, you can enhance your ability to lead with resilience and inclusivity.

❖ DESIGN YOUR SPHERE OF INFLUENCE

In today's rapidly evolving business landscape, designing your leadership journey involves more than just individual growth. It also requires active engagement within a community of like-minded leaders. By participating in training webinars and networking groups, for instance, you can access valuable insights and strategies that enhance your ability to motivate and manage teams as well as foster a resilient and inclusive work environment. These platforms offer practical guidance on improving team performance and navigating the complexities of modern leadership.

One powerful example of such a community is The Joyful Leader Launchpad, an insight to action executive mastermind group. This exclusive network offers leaders a unique opportunity to connect virtually, reducing the isolation often felt at the top. Facilitated by licensed behavioral health clinicians and experienced executive coaches, the group dives into critical topics including hiring, managing, and identifying toxic or apathetic employees while also providing essential advice on fundraising, maintaining integrity, and adapting to the fast-paced business landscape. This supportive environment allows leaders to share challenges, exchange ideas, and learn best practices for reestablishing company culture, especially in a hybrid work setting.

Mastermind groups are more than just traditional networking groups; they're dynamic platforms where leadership and innovation converge. By selecting topics that align with your specific needs, you can engage in discussions that directly address your challenges, whether it's navigating staffing issues, ensuring inclusivity for new hires, or fostering team flexibility. These spaces are designed to empower you to present your authentic professional self, gain valuable perspectives, and contribute to a collective journey of growth and learning. Ultimately, they enable you to lead with greater confidence, resilience, and purpose.

To build an inclusive culture through a mastermind group, focus on actively engaging with people as they are, acknowledging their unique differences, and fostering an environment where everyone feels they truly belong. This involves actively listening to diverse perspectives, modeling inclusive leadership, and embedding inclusivity into your company's core values. As Thomas Easley emphasizes, "Inclusion isn't just about changing the numbers; it's about shifting how the organization operates so that everyone feels they can bring their whole self to work." Similarly, Jeff Hoffman notes, "Inclusion isn't just about having diverse teams; it's about ensuring every voice is heard and valued, which drives true innovation."

Creating an inclusive culture is a continuous journey that requires commitment, effort, and intentionality. By listening to diverse voices, modeling inclusive leadership, and embedding inclusivity into your company's DNA, you can build a work environment where everyone thrives. Here are some tips on how to set the stage for an inclusive culture:

➢ Actively listen to diverse perspectives through consistent open forums or feedback sessions. Routinely hold interactive discussions and review forums where employees can share their thoughts and ideas in a safe space.

Ensuring every voice is genuinely heard and respected drives innovation, which is essential for maintaining a competitive edge. In my experience leading a team of transformation culture advocates, these sessions were instrumental in making our organization stand out.

➤ Model inclusive leadership by demonstrating open-mindedness, empathy, and approachability. Training your employees on unconscious bias is crucial for informed decision-making. I've done this by facilitating workshops and webinars on culture change, work–life balance, and mental health and establishing a leadership development program that achieved a 96% success rate. A focus on inclusive leadership was key to our success.

➤ Embed inclusivity into company values as a core aspect of your organization's mission and values, and clearly communicate this commitment through your policies and practices. With over a decade of experience in managing corporate culture change, for instance, I've prioritized embedding inclusivity into company values. As an author, thought leader, and developer and instructor of educational programs, I strive to ensure inclusivity is deeply woven into daily operations and foster a genuine sense of belonging.

➤ Foster a culture of respect and belonging and encourage a work environment where every employee feels respected and valued for who they are. Acknowledge and celebrate differences and ensure that organizational practices are inclusive of all backgrounds. This allows everyone to bring their professionally authentic whole selves to work. I did this myself while leading mental well-being initiatives at CVS Health. Working closely with teams with diverse ways of thinking, I helped to promote a culture of respect and inclusion that aligned with corporate social responsibility goals.

➢ Establish and support employee resource groups (commonly referred to as "ERGs"), which provide platforms for distinct groups to share their experiences and influence company decisions. This strategy not only supports inclusivity but also empowers employees to take an active role in shaping the organizational culture. When I did this, I created and developed a team of behavioral health culture advocates who communicated culture initiatives to our management team. In doing so, I spearheaded cultural change initiatives that impacted over 300,000 employees. Through supporting ERGs we were able to create a more inclusive and engaged workforce where employees felt empowered to take an active role in shaping the culture of the company.

❖ DESIGN YOUR CONNECTIONS

In the world of business, connections are not just casual interactions; they're the building blocks of opportunity. Turning connections into business opportunities requires a strategic approach that goes beyond an initial handshake or introduction. It's about engaging meaningfully with others, understanding their needs, and finding ways to create mutual value. When done right, each connection has the potential to open new doors and propel your business forward.

One of the key elements in transforming connections into opportunities is the power of follow-up. It's not enough to simply meet someone and exchange business cards; you need to maintain and nurture that relationship over time. This means being consistent and strategic in your follow-ups, whether they're through a quick email, a phone call, or even a coffee (tea for me) meeting. By staying present through this top-of-mind awareness, you keep the connection alive and position yourself as a valuable resource when the right opportunity arises.

Another critical factor is aligning your offerings with the needs and values of your potential partners or clients. This requires active listening and a deep understanding of their business objectives. When you demonstrate how your services or products can solve their problems or enhance their operations, you create a compelling reason for them to engage with you further. This alignment is not just about selling; it's about building trust and showing that you're invested in their success.

Emotional intelligence plays a crucial role in this process. Understanding and managing your own emotions while also being attuned to the emotions of others allows you to navigate conversations and relationships more effectively. It's about recognizing when to push forward, when to pull back, and how to communicate in a way that resonates with the other person. This skill is essential not just in business but in all aspects of life because it helps build stronger, more authentic connections.

Finally, never underestimate the power of positive intentions. Approaching each interaction with a genuine desire to help and create value can lead to unexpected opportunities. People are drawn to those who are sincere, trustworthy, and operate with integrity. I didn't realize my superpower of being a connector until I was asked to speak and moderate a panel at the 2024 Diversity Alliance for Science East Coast Conference. The invitation came directly from the president, who had witnessed firsthand my unique brand of networking and connecting with corporate leaders and entrepreneurs. She recognized that my approach was not only effective but also genuine, supportive, and uplifting, a combination that resonated with people across various industries. This experience was a turning point for me because it highlighted the significance of connection in creating business opportunities and fostering growth.

❖ DESIGN YOUR QUESTIONS

As you consider your own connections, I encourage you to explore questions you can ask leaders in your network to deepen those relationships and uncover new avenues for growth. When speaking with leaders, it's vital to be prepared with the right questions. Here are five I have found to be effective:

1. What do you stand for? If you had to do a TED Talk today, what would it be about?
2. What did you do to get to where you are today? How did you become successful?
3. What is your definition of leadership? How do you show up as a leader in various capacities (e.g., leader of people, customers, team, or those in higher positions)?
4. What three principles do you live by?
5. How do you motivate people?

When you apply these insights alongside the strategies we've discussed, you build a powerful framework for turning every connection into a potential business breakthrough.

TAKE INSIGHT INTO ACTION

Now that we've explored the transformative power of getting Set, let's shift our focus to fostering a culture of lasting joy with unique, impactful, and practical strategies that can make an enduring impact. Whether you're looking to create a joyful and supportive work environment, build strategic alliances, or position yourself for leadership opportunities, these next steps will guide you towards further empowering your growth and success.

> ➤ **Foster a Culture of Lasting Joy: The Impact of Resilience Gift Boxes**
>
> Resilience Gift Boxes are powerful tools to support event attendees on their journey of healing and self-discovery. Each box is thoughtfully curated to introduce the concept of resilience and encourage individuals to dive deeper into its practice. By providing tangible resources and inspiration, these gift boxes serve as a catalyst for personal growth and reflection, empowering attendees to continue the important work they've begun. They are designed not only to inspire and motivate but also to acknowledge and congratulate the effort and progress each person has made.
>
> When leaders surprise their employees with a Resilience Gift Box, they create an atmosphere of joy and recognition, optimizing the employee experience and fostering engagement. From seeing an employee smile while reading a personalized greeting card from their leader to watching them discover the carefully selected gifts and inspirational messages within, the excitement of receiving these boxes is palpable. A CEO of a marketing company who gifted these boxes to their staff

shared how the experience brought smiles to everyone's faces, especially during a challenging time following layoffs. The careful selection of these boxes alleviated stress and served as a beautiful expression of the leader's care and appreciation. These small tokens are lasting reminders of resilience that offer comfort and encouragement long after an event has ended.

➤ **Gain Political Support: Access Power from an Internal Mentor**

A mentor can support you in navigating the political currents and "shoulds" of an organization. Ideally, the culture should not be political because many people don't want to engage or judge the political environment. Still, it's important to be aware of politics within your organization and determine the best way to navigate your career growth given the climate. Begin by asking yourself two questions:

1. What will be my path to access some of that power?

2. Which relationships will help me shape the type of career that will give me the maximum ability to fulfill my talents?

➤ **Lead From Where You Are**

To demonstrate that you're ready for a leadership position, it's crucial to begin by leading from your current role. Start leading from where you are, and somehow doors begin to open. Adopting this mindset shifts your focus from waiting for opportunities to actively creating them. By taking initiative, showcasing your skills, and making strategic decisions, you position yourself as a natural leader in the eyes of others.

➤ Ways to Demonstrate You're Ready for a Leadership Position

- *Build financial and business acumen.*
  Financial and business acumen is essential for leadership readiness. Beyond just understanding numbers, it's about interpreting what those numbers tell you and reading the story behind the numbers to make sound decisions based on that information. Develop this skill by focusing on analyzing financial reports, understanding market trends, and recognizing patterns that could impact your organization. Engage in decision-making processes where you can practice making quick, yet informed judgments. Kelvin McLaurin suggests that leaders should be able to make decisions swiftly and be adaptable enough to change course if needed. This knowledge empowers you to make informed choices and demonstrate your value in more significant ways.

- *Strengthen project and initiative management.*
  Effective project management is a key indicator of leadership readiness. Successful leaders can manage complex projects, navigate challenges, and deliver results. It involves not only managing timelines and resources but also navigating challenges and aligning projects with broader organizational goals. Enhance this skill by taking ownership of a project from start to finish, ensuring you track progress, communicate effectively with stakeholders, and adjust plans as necessary. Demonstrating your ability to lead initiatives and deliver results highlights your capability of taking on more significant leadership roles. By mastering

these skills, you also build a track record of success that others will notice.

- *Build organizational savvy and engage the right people to help you be successful.*
  Organizational savvy is about understanding the landscape of your organization and knowing how to get things done efficiently within it. The most successful leaders know how to navigate their organizational landscape, align with key stakeholders, and leverage their networks. Judgment in decision-making often involves engaging the right people who complement your strengths. Cultivate relationships with these people and learn how to leverage their expertise to fill gaps in your own knowledge. This approach increases your effectiveness and positions you as a leader who knows how to navigate complex situations and build strong, collaborative teams.

- *Focus on increased autonomy and decision-making.*
  Leaders are often distinguished by their ability to make decisions independently and with confidence. Yet there needs to be a balance between making quick decisions and taking the time needed for thorough analysis. To demonstrate readiness for leadership, seek opportunities where you can exercise autonomy in your role. Practice making decisions that consider both short-term needs and long-term impacts and be prepared to adapt if the outcome isn't as expected. This ability to make sound, timely decisions will show that you're ready to take on more significant responsibility, paving the way for new leadership.

➤ Advance Your Career Through Succession Planning

- *Understand succession planning.*
  Succession planning is a critical tool for advancing your career because it involves preparing yourself for future leadership roles within your organization. To effectively leverage succession planning, start by gaining a deep understanding of the process within your company. This includes identifying the skills and experiences that are valued for advancement and aligning your development goals accordingly. Engage with your manager or HR department to discuss your career aspirations and seek feedback on how to position yourself as a candidate for future roles.

- *Map out your career path in a way that aligns with organizational growth and departmental expansion plans.*
  Understanding the succession process also means being aware of the opportunities available beyond your current position. Research typical career trajectories within your organization and identify the roles that align with your skills and interests. By mapping out potential career paths, you can proactively seek out experiences, projects, or mentorships that will prepare you for these next steps. This strategic approach ensures that when opportunities arise, you're considered a top candidate.

- *Identify and nurture future leaders.*
  For leaders, finding the right successor is a crucial aspect of ensuring the continuity and success of an organization. When looking for a successor,

it's important to identify individuals who not only possess the necessary technical skills but also demonstrate strong leadership qualities. Look for candidates who exhibit strategic thinking, adaptability, and a strong understanding of the organization's values and goals. These individuals should be proactive in their roles, consistently seeking to improve and take on new challenges.

- *Evaluate interpersonal skills and growth potential.*
Consider a potential successor's ability to build relationships and influence others. A great leader drives results while inspiring and motivating their team. Look for someone who can effectively communicate, collaborate across departments, and foster a positive work culture. It's also essential to assess their willingness to learn and grow, because the best successors are those who are committed to continuous development and can evolve alongside the organization.

- *Prepare your successors through mentorship and developmental opportunities.*
Involve potential successors in key projects and decision-making processes to gauge their readiness and provide them with opportunities to demonstrate their capabilities. By actively mentoring and supporting them, you help ensure that when the time comes, they're fully prepared to step into the leadership role and drive the organization forward. This proactive approach to succession planning secures the future of the organization and nurtures the next generation of leaders.

➤ **Empower Continuous Learning and Growth**

A resilient and engaged workforce is needed to meet objectives, accomplish organizational goals, and over-deliver to customers. Leaders who prioritize ongoing development create an environment where employees feel valued, supported, and inspired to reach their full potential. This not only enhances individual skills but also contributes to the collective success of the organization.

To implement this, leaders can encourage a growth mindset by doing three things:

1. Provide access to training programs, workshops, and mentoring opportunities.

2. Give feedback often and personalize development plans to help employees identify their strengths and areas for improvement, which fosters a culture of self-improvement and innovation.

3. Nurture an atmosphere in which learning is celebrated and mistakes are seen as opportunities for growth.

Through these measures, leaders can cultivate a team that is adaptable, motivated, and committed to achieving long-term success.

➤ **Build Strategic Alliances**

Whether within your organization or among external partners, strategic alliances are crucial for driving innovation, expanding influence, and achieving shared goals. Leaders can establish these alliances by identifying common objectives and aligning efforts with others who share a similar vision. Building trust and open communication is fundamental to these partnerships because doing so ensures all parties feel heard, respected, and invested in the outcome.

Strategic alliances both strengthen your position and bring diverse perspectives and resources to the table, all of which enhance your ability to navigate challenges and seize new opportunities. Here are some steps you can take to build strategic alliances:

1. Identify potential partners.

   Seek out internal and external stakeholders whose goals and values align with your organization's vision. Look for opportunities where collaboration can lead to mutual benefits.

2. Build trust through open communication.

   Establish regular communication with potential allies. Be transparent about your objectives and encourage them to share their own. This will build a foundation of trust and cooperation.

3. Define clear objectives and roles.

   When forming alliances, ensure that all parties clearly understand the shared goals and their roles in achieving them. This helps maintain focus and accountability throughout the partnership.

4. Leverage diverse perspectives.

   Encourage a culture of openness where diverse perspectives are valued. Diversity of thought comes from different generations, varying levels within the organization, and contrasting expertise and cultural backgrounds. Being open to receiving feedback from those with diverse perspectives leads to innovative solutions and stronger outcomes for all parties involved.

5. Evaluate and strengthen alliances.
   Regularly assess the effectiveness of your strategic alliances. Look for ways to deepen relationships, resolve any issues, and ensure that all parties continue to benefit from the collaboration.

By strategically collaborating with others, leaders can amplify their impact, drive positive change, and create more connected and supportive work environments. This approach supports individual and organizational growth and contributes to a broader culture of joy, cooperation, and shared success.

KEANE INSIGHT: Building resilience and success starts with shaping your landscape: nurturing relationships, mentors, networks, and your leadership brand. Remember to lead from where you are, no matter where you are or what circumstances you're in. By fostering trust and open communication, you'll naturally strengthen your influence and alliances. Take time to regularly reflect and adjust, ensuring you stay on course while creating a culture of joy and growth.

In this chapter, we explored how getting set lays the foundation for resilience and success by carefully designing key aspects of your life and career, from your landscape and mentors to your network, employees, and leadership brand. With these elements in place, you're now prepared to thrive and lead with impact. But setting the stage is only the beginning. In the next chapter, we'll focus on taking action. We'll explore how getting going enhances our resilience and success and we'll plan how to get you moving forward to deliver on your goals. It's time to put your plans into motion. With that in mind, ask yourself, "Who will I connect with today?"

Team Resilience Gift Boxes

Inspire team resilience and motivation with curated items designed to create an atmosphere that supports well-being, celebrates progress, encourages personal growth, and enhances joy and employee engagement.

CHAPTER 9

GO

Did you hear about the runner who got teased?
She took it all in stride.

~John Brueckner, *World's Greatest Dad Jokes*

N ow that you've laid the groundwork by setting your foundation, it's time to move from planning to action. This is where real progress begins. The Go stage is a critical part of the resilience model because it's when you transition from vision to execution and turn your carefully designed plans into tangible outcomes. This stage is about momentum, determination, and resilience. It's where the strategies you've developed start to unfold and where your commitment to your goals is truly tested.

Delivering on your goals requires more than just effort; it demands a clear understanding of the steps you need to take and the ability to adapt as challenges arise. The KEANE INSIGHTS Approach™—encompassing Knowledge, Empathy, Accountability, New perspectives, Engagement, Innovative ideas, Next-level Solutions, Inspiration, Guidance, Healthy culture, Teamwork, and Success—serves as your roadmap. These elements are designed to help you get Going, and they sustain the drive needed to achieve long-term success.

As we explore how getting Going enhances our resilience and success and how the KEANE INSIGHTS Approach can guide you, remember that this is where the real work begins. It's time to take the insights you've gained and put them into action, step by step, to deliver on your goals and make your vision a reality.

HOW GETTING GOING ENHANCES OUR RESILIENCE AND SUCCESS

The Go stage of the resilience model is often where many people and organizations find themselves stuck. I've seen countless individuals and teams I've worked with excel at getting Ready and be strong at getting Set, but when it comes to actually getting Going, they falter. They have everything they need and feel fully prepared, yet they struggle to put it all into action. The real challenge lies in moving from preparation to execution.

This stage is where momentum meets action, and it's crucial for finding joy, reducing stress, and building resilience. When we move from planning to doing, we unlock a sense of accomplishment that brings us joy and satisfaction. As Liza Rossi shares, "Tapping into your own joy propels the resilience journey." This joy originates from within, is fueled by our internal growth, and is expressed externally through the impact of our actions. Resilience acts as the vehicle that carries this inner joy out into the world, where it's reflected in the progress we make and the positive impact we create.

Consider the story of an entrepreneur who spent months meticulously planning the launch of a new product. They had everything in place—market research, a strong team, and a detailed strategy—yet fear of failure kept them from taking that final step. As a result, the product never launched, and the entrepreneur's potential joy and success remained unrealized. In contrast, another entrepreneur with a similar plan took the plunge despite uncertainties. By getting going, they not only launched the product but also found joy in the process and built resilience by learning from each challenge they encountered.

When we fail to get going, we often find ourselves stuck in a cycle of stress and frustration that leaves us feeling overwhelmed by the sheer volume of what needs to be done. But taking that first step, even if small, reduces stress by breaking down tasks into manageable actions. As Rossi mentioned, "The stress of responsibility can be overwhelming, but the more I worked on my internal resilience, the better I managed it." Taking action transforms anxiety into productivity, empowering us to move forward with confidence. In essence, the Go stage is about taking action in order to create a life and career filled with joy, resilience, and success. It's the moment when you move from preparation to execution while embracing the challenges and rewards that come with it.

As we explore the importance of taking action, it's essential to have a guiding framework that supports this journey. This is where the KEANE INSIGHTS Approach comes into play. It offers a comprehensive strategy to help you get Going and achieve your goals. By focusing on the intersection of who you are and what you do, this approach ensures that your internal strengths are aligned with your external actions and are leading to meaningful progress. Let's explore how this approach can ignite your path forward and give you confidence and a sense of purpose.

THE KEANE INSIGHTS APPROACH

There is an intersection between who you are and what you do, and in the middle of that intersection are KEANE INSIGHTS that empower leaders to build resilient, mentally healthy, and highly productive organizations that are ready to meet the demands of the modern workplace.

True resilience lays the foundation for a healthy, productive workplace. When leaders cultivate mental wellness, they unlock the potential for greater productivity, both for themselves and their teams. This is where the model Ready, Set, Go comes into play, and it's represented by three overlapping circles: resilience, mental wellness, and productivity. These elements are interconnected, as resilience drives mental wellness, which in turn fuels productivity.

The Power of Joy™

As a leader, reducing stress and burnout is crucial to your success. By transforming your thought processes and expanding your perspectives, you can elevate your effectiveness and directly impact service, development, and leadership. This growth will help you navigate the constant changes in the workplace and drive better company profitability. Keane Insights offers a comprehensive approach that blends practical knowledge with emotional intelligence, enabling you to transform your organization from the inside out. The elements of the approach give you access to tools and strategies designed to help you excel in your role as a professional, corporate leader, or entrepreneur. Through actions such as fostering knowledge, demonstrating empathy, holding accountability, and introducing new ways to engage your teams, you can create an environment where innovation and success thrive.

The KEANE INSIGHTS Approach is built on 12 key pillars:

1. Knowledge
2. Empathy
3. Accountability
4. New perspectives
5. Engagement
6. Innovative ideas
7. Next-level Solutions
8. Inspiration
9. Guidance
10. Healthy culture

11. Teamwork

12. Success

These elements help you build a resilient, mentally healthy, and highly productive organization that is ready to meet the demands of the modern workplace. Let's take a closer look and walk through the pillars step by step.

KNOWLEDGE

Knowledge is the cornerstone of achieving organizational goals. It provides leaders with the insights necessary to navigate complex challenges. By understanding market trends, employee dynamics, and customer needs, leaders can establish realistic targets and develop strategies that drive success. This knowledge is vital for building resilience because it enables leaders to adapt to change and sustain momentum even in challenging times. For instance, when launching our eLearning course called "Growing Your Resilience," Keane Insights collaborated with a marketing firm to conduct thorough market research, analyze competitors, and define the ideal client and market strategy. This strategic approach ensures that we effectively reach our target audience, demonstrating the power of informed decision-making.

A key takeaway is to stay updated with industry trends and promote continuous learning within your team. A well-informed team is capable of overcoming obstacles and capitalizing on opportunities.

EMPATHY

Empathy plays a crucial role in achieving long-term success by fostering strong relationships with both employees and customers. When leaders understand the needs and motivations of others, they can make decisions that resonate throughout their organizations, which leads to higher engagement and satisfaction. Empathy also contributes to resilience by building trust and connection, which is essential in challenging times. Leaders who demonstrate empathy can better support their teams and maintain morale, helping the organization persevere.

A practical tip is to practice active listening and encourage open communication. This approach builds a resilient, loyal community that supports business goals. For example, during the peak of the COVID-19 pandemic, I led a virtual support group program for employees who were struggling with isolation and stress. By actively listening and fostering open communication, I helped create a strong sense of community and trust among remote teams. This empathetic leadership not only preserved employee morale but increased productivity and job satisfaction, showcasing the profound impact of empathy in leadership.

ACCOUNTABILITY

Accountability is crucial for achieving organizational goals because it ensures that every individual takes responsibility for their actions. When leaders and teams hold themselves accountable, it creates a clear and direct path towards meeting objectives. This culture of accountability also bolsters resilience by fostering trust and reliability within the organization. During times of crisis, knowing that everyone is committed to their responsibilities helps keep the organization on course.

A practical approach is to set clear expectations and regularly review progress, which reinforces trust and resilience across teams. For entrepreneurs, having an accountability partner is especially valuable in reaching your goals as a CEO. An accountability partner who shares your principles, outlook, and work ethic can provide the support you need to stay focused on your goals and action steps. This partnership helps mitigate the isolation that can come with being at the helm of your organization, ensuring you remain aligned with your objectives.

NEW PERSPECTIVES

Embracing new ways of thinking is essential for driving innovation and maintaining a competitive edge. Fresh perspectives often lead to breakthrough ideas that can fuel business growth. This openness to new approaches is also a key factor in building resilience because it enables organizations to pivot quickly in response to challenges. At Keane Insights, we introduced innovative brainstorming sessions that encouraged vendors to think outside the box. This approach resulted in the development of a novel service offering that opened a new market segment for the company. Fostering a culture of innovation and welcoming unconventional ideas positioned the organization to stay ahead of the competition and remain resilient in the face of industry changes.

Throughout my career, various industries have hired me to bring fresh eyes to their challenges, whether it was in mental health, training and development, learning and performance, procurement supplier management or employee assistance programs. My ability to introduce new ways of thinking and innovative strategies has consistently helped these organizations adapt, grow, and thrive amid change.

ENGAGEMENT

Effectively engaging remote and hybrid teams and getting them to thrive is essential for maintaining productivity and collaboration, both of which are vital for achieving organizational goals. When teams feel connected and valued, they're more likely to contribute to the organization's success.

While leading a training team, I spearheaded initiatives to keep remote teams connected and engaged. Through regular virtual check-ins and creative team-building activities, I ensured that all team members felt valued and motivated. This approach was crucial in maintaining alignment and resilience across the organization. As I often say, "We *can* foster connection among remote teams!" This unity is key in helping organizations weather disruptions without losing momentum.

INNOVATIVE IDEAS

Innovative ideas are the driving force behind achieving goals in new and more efficient ways. Innovation allows organizations to solve problems creatively and capitalize on new opportunities. It also fosters resilience by enabling organizations to adapt quickly to changing circumstances. When challenges arise, innovative thinking leads to solutions that keep an organization moving forward.

A practical tip is to encourage a culture of curiosity and experimentation. Reward team members for bringing forward new ideas and be willing to pilot them even if they involve some risk. By demonstrating openness to experimentation and learning from failures, you empower your team to explore new possibilities and drive innovation.

NEXT-LEVEL SOLUTIONS

Implementing new solutions is crucial for overcoming obstacles and achieving business objectives. New solutions often involve leveling up by integrating technology, optimizing processes, or redefining strategies to better meet goals, and they're a cornerstone of resilience because they enable organizations to respond effectively to challenges and ensure continuity and success, even in the face of adversity. Staying open to technological advancements and regularly reviewing operations to identify areas where new solutions can enhance efficiency is key to maintaining a high level of resilience and success.

While working with a learning and performance team, I noticed that people frequently returned for retraining on a new platform. Through conversations with the learners, I discovered that they had forgotten how to use the platform by the time it went live. To address this, I implemented a virtual environment called "Beyond the Classroom," where learners could continue practicing and reinforcing their skills until the system went live, which included scenarios, practice environments, videos, workflows, and more. This solution not only enhanced their learning experience but also ensured they were fully prepared, which ultimately contributed to increased efficiency and effectiveness within the organization.

INSPIRATION

Inspiration motivates teams to strive for excellence and reach their full potential, which is crucial for achieving organizational goals. When leaders inspire their teams, they create a shared vision that drives everyone towards common objectives. Inspiration also plays a significant role in building resilience because it instills a sense of purpose and determination that helps teams push through challenges.

A practical tip is to regularly share success stories and celebrate achievements. This approach helps inspire your team by showing them the impact of their work and the possibilities that lie ahead. For example, as a board member of Experience Camps for Grieving Children, I regularly share success stories of the children and celebrate their achievements along their journey. This practice uplifts the team, reinforces the impact of our work, and shows the possibilities that lie ahead.

GUIDANCE

Effective guidance is essential for fostering both individual and team growth. By aligning development efforts with the organization's goals, you ensure that everyone is well-equipped to contribute to the company's overall success. Guidance also plays a crucial role in building resilience because it provides direction and stability during uncertain times. With clear and consistent guidance, teams can confidently navigate challenges and maintain forward momentum.

As a mentor to CEOs and individual contributors in various settings, I've strived to provide regular feedback that helps my mentees develop the skills and confidence they need to secure both internal and external job offers. This both fosters individual growth and aligns with the organization's objectives, ultimately contributing to long-term success.

HEALTHY CULTURE

A healthy culture cultivates an environment where employees are motivated, engaged, and dedicated to achieving organizational goals. It encourages collaboration and innovation, both of which are critical for success. A strong culture is the foundation of resilience because it supports well-being and performance and allows an organization to thrive even in difficult times.

As I tend to say, "One of the best parts of being a leader is creating an inspiring culture." By investing in employee well-being programs and promoting work–life balance, you can build a healthy culture rooted in trust, respect, and mutual support.

TEAMWORK

Teamwork is essential for achieving complex goals that require collaboration across different areas of the organization. When teams work well together, they can tackle challenges more effectively and achieve better results. Teamwork also builds resilience by creating a support network within an organization. Teams that collaborate well are better equipped to handle stress and adapt to change.

Foster teamwork by creating an environment of open communication and mutual respect and encourage cross-functional collaboration to break down silos and build strong, resilient teams. This approach works exceptionally well when leading cross-functional collaborations because it increases the opportunity for successful resolution of challenges related to launching a new product or service. By fostering teamwork, Keane Insights has not only helped organizations overcome obstacles but also contributed to the well-being and resilience of their employees, which ultimately leads to better outcomes.

SUCCESS

Success is the ultimate goal of any organization, and it's achieved through consistent delivery of results that align with the organization's objectives. When all pillars of the KEANE INSIGHTS Approach come together, success follows. Resilience is the foundation of long-term success, ensuring that organizations can withstand setbacks and continue moving towards their goals regardless of the obstacles they face.

Define clear success metrics and regularly review progress, celebrating small wins along the way to maintain momentum and reinforce the behaviors that lead to success.

The KEANE INSIGHTS Approach to taking action is centered on empowering leaders and teams to align their internal strengths with strategic objectives, ensuring that every effort is directed towards meaningful progress. By combining knowledge, empathy, accountability, and innovative thinking, our method transforms challenges into opportunities for growth and success. We can then focus on fostering resilience through effective guidance, teamwork, and a healthy culture, enabling organizations to not only meet their goals but to thrive in the face of adversity.

Let's explore the steps to make that happen.

GET GOING TO DELIVER ON YOUR GOALS

Achieving your goals requires not just setting them but following through on them with consistent action, self-awareness, and adaptability to challenges along the way. To truly deliver on your objectives, it's important to tap into your internal resources of joy and resilience while also strategically designing your path forward. Here are some actionable steps to help you get Going and stay on track towards reaching your goals:

❖ GET GOING BY TAPPING INTO YOUR JOY

As we've seen, joy is a powerful motivator that can sustain your energy and enthusiasm over the long haul. By tapping into what genuinely brings you joy, you can maintain positive momentum even when the journey gets tough. To do this, identify activities or aspects of your work that genuinely bring you joy. Whether it's collaborating with a team, problem-solving, or creating something new, focusing on these activities will keep your energy high. And starting your day with joy-infused tasks sets a positive tone and creates a ripple effect that boosts your productivity and creativity throughout the day.

When you lead with joy, you're more likely to maintain enthusiasm and drive, even in the face of challenges. It helps to create a "joy list" of tasks you look forward to and ensure they're a regular part of your routine. This list will be your go-to for maintaining motivation and energy and helping you navigate through even the most challenging days.

1. Think about the tasks and activities in your life and work that genuinely bring you happiness.

2. Reflect on the aspects of your job that make you feel most engaged and fulfilled. Consider moments when you feel energized and excited, whether it's collaborating with your team, solving complex problems, or engaging in creative projects.

3. Write down these activities as the first step in building your joy list.

4. Review your list and prioritize these joyful tasks by incorporating them into your daily routine.

5. Aim to start your day with one of these joy-inducing activities to set a positive tone and boost your energy for the rest of the day. By intentionally placing these tasks at the beginning of your schedule, you create a ripple

effect that enhances your productivity and creativity throughout the day.

6. Make it a habit to regularly update your joy list.

As you grow and your work evolves, new activities that bring you joy may emerge, while others may shift in importance. By keeping your list current, you ensure that you're always tapping into the activities that sustain your enthusiasm and drive, helping you navigate challenges with a positive and resilient mindset.

❖ GET GOING BY MAINTAINING YOUR MOMENTUM

Stress is inevitable, but it doesn't have to derail your progress. By finding joy even in stressful moments, you can maintain your momentum and continue moving forward. When stress builds up, take a moment to shift your perspective. Focus on the small wins and the progress you've made, no matter how minor they seem. By recognizing and celebrating these small victories, you're able to reframe stress as an opportunity for growth rather than a hindrance. Here is a practice to help you maintain a balanced perspective and ensure joy remains a constant presence in your life:

- ✓ Incorporate gratitude into your daily routine to further enhance your ability to find joy under pressure.
- ✓ Pause and reflect on what's going well during particularly stressful moments.
- ✓ Write down a few things you're thankful for, even if they're small.
- ✓ Ask yourself what aspects of your life and work bring you joy and how you can incorporate more of these elements into your daily routine.

Shifting your focus to positive aspects during stressful times and reflecting on what's going well helps in reframing challenges as opportunities, which in turn allows you to keep pushing forward without losing steam and find joy in the midst of pressure. This reframing is crucial for maintaining a positive outlook and staying on course. Use stress as a signal to pause, recalibrate, and find joy in the process rather than just focusing on the outcome.

❖ GET GOING BY EMBRACING CHALLENGES

Resilience is the cornerstone of long-term success. By embracing challenges rather than avoiding them, you build the strength and adaptability needed to overcome obstacles and keep moving towards your goals. View challenges as opportunities to build your resilience. Instead of shying away from difficult tasks, tackle them head-on with the mindset that overcoming them will make you stronger. This proactive approach turns your challenges into stepping stones for growth.

✓ Break down challenges into smaller, actionable tasks. This approach makes them less daunting and helps you build confidence as you progress.

✓ Remind yourself of past successes when you've overcome similar challenges to reinforce your resilience and help you maintain focus and determination.

✓ Create a "resilience toolkit" filled with strategies and resources you can turn to when facing challenges. Having these tools readily available will help you stay grounded and resilient and enable you to push through obstacles and continue progressing towards your goals with confidence. Here are some things you can add to your kit:

- Stress management techniques
- Support network of colleagues or mentors
- Reminders of past achievements.

Directly tackling challenges strengthens your ability to cope with future difficulties and enhances your confidence, both of which make you more capable of achieving your goals.

❖ GET GOING BY ALIGNING YOURSELF WITH YOUR GOALS

Self-awareness is key to setting and achieving goals that are truly meaningful to you. By understanding who you are at your core and what drives you, you can ensure that your goals align with your true self. This makes it easier to stay motivated and on track and enables you to set goals that are both achievable and genuinely fulfilling. Here are some tips for doing this:

- ✓ Take time to reflect on your strengths, values, and passions.
- ✓ Consider what drives you and what aspects of your work resonate most deeply with your personal values.
- ✓ Regularly assess whether your current goals align with your evolving self. As you grow and change, your goals should evolve with you.
- ✓ Schedule regular self-reflection sessions through actions such as journaling to explore whether your goals still reflect your true self. This practice helps ensure that your efforts are always directed towards what truly matters to you.

✓ Use your self-awareness to make informed decisions about your career and personal life.

When your goals are aligned with your authentic self, you're more likely to pursue them with passion and persistence. This alignment not only increases your chances of success but also ensures that the path you're on is one that brings you genuine satisfaction and joy. By staying true to yourself, you create a fulfilling and purpose-driven life.

❖ GET GOING BY STRUCTURING YOUR JOURNEY

Just as a well-planned landscape ensures a garden's growth, a well-designed plan ensures your success. By visualizing your path and regularly adjusting it, you create a clear roadmap that guides your efforts towards achieving your goals. This visualization process helps you see the bigger picture and ensures that all aspects of your life are aligned with your objectives. To visualize the landscape of your life and career, take these simple steps:

1. Identify the elements that are already in place, what needs to change, and where you need to focus your efforts to achieve your goals.

2. Create a detailed "goal map" that acts as your guide, keeps you on track, and ensures your efforts are consistently directed towards your desired outcomes. While doing this, ask yourself these questions:

   • What specific steps do I need to take?

   • What are the resources required?

   • What are the potential obstacles?

3. Regularly review and update your goal map to reflect any changes in your circumstances or objectives, keeping it a dynamic tool that evolves with you.

Use your goal map to sustain focus and drive as you work towards your objectives. Regularly reviewing it and making necessary adjustments will keep your path to success clear and actionable, which aids in achieving your goals and ensures that the journey itself is rewarding and purposeful. With a clear vision of where you're headed and the steps required to get there, you can maintain momentum and stay on track while directing all your efforts towards reaching your desired outcomes.

TAKE INSIGHT INTO ACTION

The journey from insight to action is a transformative one, in which self-awareness and understanding help fuel meaningful change. It's about taking the wisdom and experiences you've gathered and translating them into deliberate, impactful steps in your professional life. This transition is about far more than just knowing what needs to be done; it extends to embodying the courage, clarity, and resilience to act on that knowledge.

For many, the journey starts with understanding the need to prioritize self-care and balancing that with their work life. By recognizing the importance of personal well-being, you can make decisions that align with your true purpose rather than striving for external validation. Once you achieve this internal alignment, your path to professional growth becomes clear. And when you're clear on your goals, you can focus on what's truly important: your desire to achieve. With this focus, you're more equipped to navigate significant career decisions, from job changes to managing relationships with leaders. Here are some ways you can do this:

➤ **Presenting to Leaders**

When presenting to leaders, it's essential to start with a clear understanding of the "why" behind your presentation. Leaders are often more interested in the impact your proposal or idea will have on their business than they are in the intricate details of how it works. As Robyn Hatcher emphasizes, "Nobody cares what the components of the widget are. What they care about is what the widget is going to do for them and their business."

1. Begin by identifying how your presentation aligns with the organization's goals or addresses its leaders' challenges. For example, if you're pitching a new strategy, focus on how it will enhance productivity, improve team morale, or boost profitability. By framing your presentation around these outcomes, you immediately capture leaders' attention and establish the relevance of your proposal.

2. Once you've established the why, it's crucial to structure your presentation in a way that's both engaging and informative. Incorporate stories, data, and visuals that support your main points, but always tie them back to the benefits for the organization. For instance, if you have a case study or success story, highlight how it demonstrates the effectiveness of your approach and what it could mean for the leader's specific context. This not only makes your

presentation more relatable but also helps leaders visualize the potential impact of your ideas within their organization.

3. Anticipate the questions and concerns leaders might have. Be prepared to address them confidently and demonstrate that you've thought through the potential challenges and have solutions. This proactive approach builds trust and positions you as a well-prepared and thoughtful professional.

4. As you conclude your proposal, summarize its key benefits and reinforce how it aligns with the leader's goals. Leave them with a clear understanding of the value you bring.

Presenting to leaders can be daunting, but preparation and confidence are key. By preparing both mentally and physically, you can accelerate decision-making and present your ideas with clarity and conviction. That way, you ensure your presentation is compelling, relevant, and persuasive and that it leads seamlessly to the next stages of decision-making.

➤ Managing Up: Overcoming Micromanagement

Managing up is a critical skill for navigating your career, especially when dealing with challenging dynamics such as micromanagement. Effectively managing your relationship with your manager can enhance your professional growth and ensure your contributions are recognized. The key is to establish clear communication and boundaries while demonstrating your value and readiness for advancement.

- *Set boundaries in communication by clearly articulating your role and contributions.*
  For example, if your manager frequently answers emails addressed to you, it's important to manage this behavior by setting clear boundaries. You can say, "When I copy you on emails and meetings, it's for visibility and transparency. For clarity and for continuity in relationship building, it's essential that I respond to emails addressed to me. If there's vital information that needs to be shared, please let me know directly, and I will include it in my response." This approach allows you to maintain control over your responsibilities while ensuring your manager stays informed.

- *Assert your value in a way that aligns with your responsibilities.*
  Managing up effectively includes negotiating for a promotion when your role evolves. When discussing your career progression, be clear about your expectations: "In three months, I plan to address key issues within the team, and at that point I expect a level increase and salary adjustment. Let's discuss this with HR to ensure my contributions are recognized with a next-level title and appropriate compensation." This proactive approach emphasizes that your promotion should reflect your expanded role and impact.

- *Ask the right questions to align your career goals with those of the organization.*
  An important part of managing up is asking insightful questions that align your career goals with the

organization's needs. During discussions about your future, ask your manager, "How do you assess performance?" to understand the promotion criteria. Follow up with, "How do you ensure people's ideas are heard?" to learn how innovation is valued. Finally, ask, "What capabilities do you plan to build to meet your long-term goals?" These questions demonstrate your commitment to both your personal growth and the company's success, positioning you as a strategic thinker ready for advancement.

Managing up requires confidence and the ability to assert your needs while respecting your leaders' expectations. As Elizabeth Davis notes, "I'm not afraid to ask questions . . . I'm just trying to gain additional insight and understanding to form my own opinions." Overcoming micromanagement is about communication, clarity, and establishing a balance that works for all parties.

➤ Promotions Made Easy

When seeking a promotion, initiating one-on-one conversations with your manager is essential. Clearly express your ambitions as an individual contributor and align them with the company's values. For example, you might say, "I love how much this company values inclusivity. That's why I'm here. My mentor suggested I seek sponsorship, and I would love for you to advocate for me. I'm aiming for a senior executive role and would appreciate your guidance." This direct approach signals your commitment and positions you as a proactive, growth-oriented employee.

232

In these discussions, it is crucial to showcase your accomplishments and how they've positively impacted the organization. Share specific examples of your work, such as, "I led a project that met all deadlines, held the team accountable, and exceeded targets." Providing concrete evidence of your contributions demonstrates your readiness for a higher role. If you've been perceived as "too nice," emphasize your ability to handle difficult situations and make tough decisions, reinforcing your capability to lead.

Here are some effective strategies to navigate discussions about promotions:

- *Proactively approach year-end reviews.*
  Year-end reviews are a critical time for promotion discussions, but it's important to understand that most decisions have already been made by this point. Instead of advocating for a promotion, focus on seeking clarity and future opportunities. Asking questions like, "Is there still a chance for a promotion this cycle?" or "What can I do to ensure I'm in a position for a promotion within the next six months?" shows you're committed to improvement and future success. This approach allows you to gather feedback and plan your next steps effectively.

- *Create urgency and demonstrate value.*
  As a leader, it's vital to recognize that decision-making is a key factor in reducing risk and increasing your value to the organization. If you've been the main decision-maker for some time without seeing a raise, it's appropriate to address this during your review. You might

say, "I've been making key decisions for the past six months, and I believe it's time to reevaluate my compensation." This conversation both highlights your contributions and sets the stage for salary discussions.

- *Leverage passion projects and continuous education.*
  To maintain momentum in your career, find passion projects that align with your goals and the company's needs. Having regular one-on-ones with your manager can keep your promotion goals on their radar. Express your desire for advancement, keep them informed about your contributions, and continually seek feedback. Additionally, consider interviewing for skip-level roles within or outside of your current organization. This will sharpen your interviewing skills, signal your readiness for the next level, and create a sense of urgency around your career progression.

➤ Job Change: When Is It Time to Move On?

When you find yourself feeling limited and undermined at your current place of work, it may be time to consider a job change. There are three main things to keep in mind if you're at this point:

1. The first step is to clearly understand your reasons for moving on. Reflect on your current situation and identify what you truly seek in your next position. For instance, if your current role lacks a clear path for upward growth, it's important to articulate this during job interviews. You might say, "I am looking for a job with more room for upward growth. There is no career path to grow in my current position, and that is why I am leaving." This demonstrates your

commitment to advancing your career and taking on greater responsibilities.

2. Next, consider how you can communicate the impact you've made in your previous roles and how these experiences have prepared you for new challenges. If you've attained roles in various levels within your current organization and now seek to grow in a different department, company, or level, frame your narrative around the desire to broaden your impact. You could say, "I have navigated through various departments of a large organization, which has added versatility to my career and is needed in a general management role. I am now looking for a team that is more collaborative and offers opportunities for innovation." This highlights your adaptability and readiness to contribute to a new environment.

3. Finally, express gratitude for the experiences and opportunities you've had while making it clear that you're ready for the next step in your career. Acknowledge the value of what you've accomplished in your current role, but also emphasize your eagerness to take on new challenges. For example, you might say, "I am grateful for what we have been able to accomplish together and thankful for the opportunities I have had. I learned a great deal from my current role, but now I am looking to add greater value to an organization where I can grow and make a more significant impact." This approach leaves a positive impression and shows that you're both appreciative and forward-looking as you move towards your next career opportunity.

Understanding when it's time to move on is critical. It's not just about escaping discomfort but about recognizing when your current role no longer serves your growth or aligns with your goals. Knowing when to pivot is a sign of resilience and self-awareness.

➤ Applying for Multiple Internal Roles

Applying for multiple positions within the same company can be a strategic way to maximize your chances of later landing a role that suits your skills and interests. However, it's essential to approach this process thoughtfully to ensure that your applications stand out and clearly communicate your qualifications for each role. Here is how to take action on this:

1. Start by carefully reviewing each job description to identify the key qualifications and responsibilities of each position.

   ✓ Make a list of your education and experience, emphasizing how you meet at least 80% of the qualifications for each role.

   ✓ Craft a cover letter that addresses your interest in applying to multiple positions within the company. In the letter, explain why you're well-qualified for each position, highlighting relevant skills and experiences that align with the different roles.

   ✓ Be sure to tailor your resume for each application, focusing on the aspects of your background that best match the specific requirements of each job.

2. Reach out to the company's recruiting or HR department to express your interest in the multiple positions you've applied for.

✓ Provide a brief overview of why you believe you're a strong candidate for each role, referencing your education and experience. This proactive communication can help you stand out and demonstrates your enthusiasm for working at the company.

✓ Ask whether there are any additional steps you should take in the application process and whether they can provide any insights into the timeline for reviewing applications.

3. One week after submitting your applications, follow up with the company or the specific department to inquire about their status.

✓ Express your continued interest in the positions, and if you haven't been selected for an interview, ask if they'd consider an informal interview or whether they could provide feedback on your application and background.

✓ Let the recruiter know that you're very interested in working for the company and would appreciate being kept in mind for future opportunities that align with your skills and qualifications. This approach underlines your dedication and helps you build a relationship with the company for potential future openings.

By following this structured approach, you demonstrate your enthusiasm and suitability for the various positions you're interested in, which increases your likelihood of success.

KEANE INSIGHT: One of the easiest ways to deliver on your goals and enhance resilience is to align yourself with what truly brings you joy. Take time to embrace challenges and turn insights into action! I like to think of it as structuring your journey: setting clear goals and tapping into your strengths. Look for ways to initiate innovative ways to meet your goals. By keeping this mindset, you not only maintain your momentum but also fuel your professional growth and success, one step at a time.

It's clear that getting Going is not just about movement but about intentional progress that enhances both resilience and success. By embracing the KEANE INSIGHTS Approach, you equip yourself and your teams to thrive. Whether it's delivering on your goals, maintaining momentum, or embracing challenges, the key is to align your actions with your broader objectives and structure your journey to support sustained progress. The insights we've explored offer practical tools for navigating career decisions, whether it's deciding when to move on from a job, managing up, presenting to leaders, or applying for internal promotions. While challenges may arise, remember that with persistence and a positive mindset, these tools can empower you to overcome obstacles and achieve your goals.

Individual Executive Coaching:
Personalized coaching sessions tailored to deepen self- awareness, enhance leadership skills, and build resilience for lasting
personal and professional growth.

Consulting and Workshops:
Strategic services offering expert guidance and actionable tools
to help teams and organizations achieve goals, strengthen resilience, and drive sustainable success.

CONCLUSION

Stress, burnout, and the process of growing resilience is easy to talk about. It's easy to make a list, and it's easy to hear what we need to do. It's the doing it part that's hard. Some of us have really big mountains we're trying to climb, and I recognize that often it's easier said than done.

I want you to really take in what you've read. You deserve joy. You deserve to live. You're entitled to live a life that lights you up. It's okay to go find what serves you. Once you can see yourself in the full glory of who you already are—your essence—and who you can become, you'll begin to live more freely, courageously loving yourself.

When I was a little girl, I wanted to dance. I have wanted to dance my entire life, and dance has been one of my greatest joys. There were many times when something stood in the way, whether an injury or somebody who was better than me, and I didn't make the cut and was left feeling like I wasn't good enough. I could have quit. I could have given up. I could have let those voices tell me it doesn't matter. But I let each one of those experiences strengthen me, and they made me stronger. Every one of those times I didn't make it helped build me up for the times I did.

Whatever it is for you, whatever it is you love and brings you real joy, prioritize it. Your joy is hiding in the places you think you don't have time for. It's behind the curtain, waiting for you to discover it, to bring it into the light. If you do nothing else, I encourage you to go back, grab whatever brings you joy by the hands and dance. Find that activity that moves you to a different mindset, then go schedule it in your calendar NOW.

Don't be scared to dance. Even if you think you're not good enough, even if you think others might not pick you, you deserve to live a life of joy. That is what resilience is all about. It's building yourself up to live *your* life to its fullest. And I hope in some way I've helped you do that. I hope you find the perfect recipe for your happily-ever-after life and beyond, and I hope you find the courage to go after it.

I'm Nicole Van Valen, helping you live the life that makes you shine. It's nice to have worked with you.

ACKNOWLEDGMENTS

To my spiritual family, especially Gary and Liza, who have dedicated their lives to sharing God's Love and Light. Your unwavering support has helped me discover my joy and has shown me how to expand it, not just in my life, but in the lives of many others. Your guidance has been a beacon that has illuminated my path.

To my parents—my first best friends, my sounding board, and my earliest examples of entrepreneurship. Mom, your grace under pressure taught me to handle life's challenges with elegance. Dad, your advice to never dim my light for anyone has been my guiding principle. Together, you have instilled in me the courage and resilience that fuel my journey.

To Alexandrea, my only daughter, who has opened my eyes to diverse perspectives. The joy and wisdom you bring into my life are beyond measure. I am deeply grateful that you chose me to be your mother.

To my husband, Dwayne, my Superman, who literally saved my life. Your love, intelligence, and support of my dreams are unmatched. The joy you have brought into my life with Andrew and Anthony is immeasurable. You are my rock and my inspiration.

To my Bahamian and Vincentian family. The love, support, and cultural heritage you have given me are the foundations upon which I stand. Our shared experiences and the way we give back to our community are embedded in my soul.

To the grieving children at Experience Camps for Grieving Children, the impoverished children at Ekukhanyeni Relief Project, and the teens facing suicidal ideation supported by the Kennedy Kids Foundation—your resilience and courage have motivated me to write this book. It is my hope that a percentage of the proceeds will support your mental health and physical well-being, providing a beacon of hope in challenging times.

To my publisher, Jenn T. Grace, who introduced me to the most harmonious experts and helped me achieve my goal of igniting a resilience movement. Your belief in my vision has been invaluable. Also to Kree Pandey, my website designer, and to Nancy Graham-Tillman, my editor and strategic developer. Together, your dedication and expertise helped turn my dream of becoming an author into reality.

EXTENDED LEARNING / WORK WITH NICOLE

❖ For additional support and resources to strengthen your resilience, be sure to visit our website at https://keaneinsights.com/. You'll find a wealth of materials, including expert articles, workshops, and downloadable guides designed to help you stay resilient in the face of challenges.

❖ Keane Insights offers a variety of additional resources that guide you in turning insight into action, empowering you to thrive both personally and professionally:

➢ Tailored to meet your leadership needs:

• If you're looking for ways to consistently apply the leadership strategies you've learned and track your progress, consider getting **The Joyful Leader Workbook™** at https://keaneinsights.com/product/the-joyful-leader-workbook/ for insights on managing stress and fostering resilience in leadership roles.

• Gain a comprehensive understanding of your resilience capacity with the **Resilience Self-Assessment** at https://keaneinsights.com/quizzes/resilience-self-assessment/ that identifies your strengths and areas for growth.

- Enhance your resilience and leadership, identify your strengths, analyze your stress triggers, and access exclusive **Reader Resources** at https://keaneinsights.com/reader-resources for transformational tools to become *The Joyful Leader*.

- For a comprehensive, self-paced development experience, enroll in our **Growing Your Resilience eLearning Training** at https://keaneinsights.com/product/growing-your-resilience/.

- Join our dynamic **Mastermind Coaching Group** at https://keaneinsights.com/services/executive-coaching/#mastermind to collaborate, share experiences, and develop effective strategies for leadership resilience.

- **Shop our merchandise** at https://keaneinsights.com/shop/ to keep resilience at the front of your mind with practical and inspiring items.

➢ Specialized resources designed to support and elevate your organization's growth and resilience:

- Engage and inspire your organization, departments, and facilities with impactful **Keynote Presentations** at https://keaneinsights.com/speaking/ that blend personal stories and actionable leadership insights.

- Participate in a **Two-Day Immersive Retreat** at https://keaneinsights.com/services/spiritual-healing/#retreats focused on resilience training, practical leadership exercises, strategic preparation, and burnout prevention.

- Participate in hands-on **Resilience Workshops and Leadership Training** at https://keaneinsights.com/services/resilience-workshops/ designed to build your resilience and enhance your leadership skills.

- Benefit from engaging with insightful **Team Engagement Video Series** content at https://keaneinsights.com/content-licensing/#video-series series that supports leadership and resilience development on a weekly basis to boost team cohesion, motivation, and collective resilience.

- Equip your organization's **Human Resources (HR)** professionals with essential tools and knowledge to support mental health in the workplace at https://keaneinsights.com/content-licensing/.

- Want to encourage team resilience? Explore our **Team Gift Boxes** at https://keaneinsights.com/gift-boxes/ as a thoughtful way to show appreciation and inspire well-being.

- **License content** at https://keaneinsights.com/content-licensing/ to enrich your organization's training programs, ensuring they meet industry standards and foster a resilient workforce.

- For tailored consulting or team workshops, explore our full suite of **Services** at https://keaneinsights.com/services/ designed to enhance organizational resilience.

246 | The Joyful Leader

Remember, building resilience is an ongoing process. By committing to continual growth through consistently applying the strategies you've learned, you'll be well on your way to becoming more resilient in both your personal and professional life. Keep up the great work! You're setting the foundation for long-term success and well-being.

NOTES

1. Liuba, "Joy vs Happiness: Their Differences and Impacts on Our Lives," Psychology, accessed July 30, 2024, https://psychology.tips/joy-vs-happiness/.

2. Barbara L. Fredrickson, "The Role of Positive Emotions in Positive Psychology: The Broaden-and-Build Theory of Positive Emotions," *American Psychologist* 56, no. 3 (2001): 218–226, https://doi.org/10.1037//0003-066x.56.3.218.

3. "Create Joy and Satisfaction," Mental Health America, accessed June 22, 2024, https://www.mhanational.org/create-joy-and-satisfaction#:~:text.

4. Kelly Carter and Anne Hawkins, "Joy at Work: Creating a Culture of Resilience," *Journal of Nursing Management* 50, no. 12 (2019): 34–42, https://doi,org/10.1097/01.NUMA.0000605156.88187.77.

5. Jennifer Aaker and Naomi Bagdonas, "How to Be Funny at Work," Harvard Business Review online, February 5, 2021, https://hbr.org/2021/02/how-to-be-funny-at-work?utm_campaign=hbr&utm_medium=social&utm_source=linkedin.

6. Karen O'Quin and Joel Aronoff, "Humor as a Technique of Social Influence," *Social Psychology Quarterly* 44, no. 4 (1981): 349–357, https://doi.org/10.2307/3033903.

7. Mayo Clinic Staff, "Stress Relief from Laughter? It's No Joke," Mayo Clinic, September 22, 2023, https://www.mayoclinic.org/healthy-lifestyle/stress-management/in-depth/stress-relief/art-20044456.

8. The Providence Heart & Vascular Team, "Amazing Ways Laughter Improves Your Heart Health," Providence, accessed June 22, 2024, https://blog.providence.org/toyourhealthblogs/amazing-ways-laughter-improves-your-heart-health.

9. JongEun Yim, "Therapeutic Benefits of Laughter in Mental Health: A Theoretical Review," *Tohoku Journal of Experimental Medicine* 239, no. 3 (2016): 243–249, https://doi.org/10.1620/tjem.239.243; NLI Staff, "The Neuroscience of Laughter, and How to Inspire More of It at Work," NeuroLeadership Institute, September 17, 2020, https://neuroleadership.com/your-brain-at-work/neuroscience-laughter-at-work/.

10. Adrián Pérez-Aranda et al., "Laughing Away the Pain: A Narrative Review of Humour, Sense of Humour and Pain," *European Journal of Pain* 23, no. 2 (2019): 220–233, https://doi.org/10.1002/ejp.1309; Dr. Barrie R. Cassileth, "Complementary Therapies in Cancer Care: Humor Therapy," CancerConnect, July 27, 2018, https://news.cancerconnect.com/treatment-care/complementary-therapies-in-cancer-care-humor-therapy.

11. Jennifer Aaker and Naomi Bagdonas, "How to Be Funny at Work," Harvard Business Review online, February 5, 2021, https://hbr.org/2021/02/

how-to-be-funny-at-work?utm_campaign=hbr&utm_medium=social&utm_source=linkedin.

12. Eric E. Vogt, Juanita Brown, and David Isaacs, *The Art of Powerful Questions: Catalyzing Insight, Innovation, and Action* (Whole Systems Associates, 2003).

13. Jessica Stillman, "A Huge New Study Reveals Most of Us Are Terrible at Choosing How We Spend Our Free Time," *Inc.*, May 19, 2022, https://www.inc.com/jessica-stillman/happiness-satisfaction-work-life-balance-leisure-activities.html.

14. Minda Zetlin, "7 Small Joys You Should Make Sure to Add to Your Daily Routine in 2022," *Inc.*, January 1, 2022, https://www.inc.com/minda-zetlin/2022-plans-goals-small-joys-daily-routine-happiness-productivity.html.

15. Adapted from "Stress Might Look Like . . . ," Positively Present, accessed May 12, 2024, https://positivelypresent.com/2014/09/23-ways-to-relax.html.

16. "What Is Burnout? 22 Signs You're Facing It (and How to Recover)," Calm, accessed June 23, 2024, https://www.calm.com/blog/beat-burnout.

17. "Burnout an 'Occupational Phenomenon': International Classification of Diseases," World Health Organization, last modified May 28, 2019, https://www.who.int/news/item/28-05-2019-burn-out-an-occupational-phenomenon-international-classification-of-diseases.

18. Gallup, Inc., *State of the Global Workplace: 2024 Report* (Gallup, Inc., 2024), https://www.gallup.com/workplace/282659/employee-burnout-perspective-paper.aspx.

19. Neil Schneiderman, Gail Ironson, and Scott D. Siegel, "Stress and Health: Psychological, Behavioral, and Biological Determinants," *Annual Review of Clinical Psychology* 1, no. 1 (2005): 607–628, https://doi.org/10.1146/annurev.clinpsy.1.102803.144141.

20. Elizabeth Perry, "Acute Stress: What You Need to Know," BetterUp, February 29, 2024, https://www.betterup.com/blog/acute-stress.

21. "Stress in America 2023: A Nation Recovering from Collective Trauma," American Psychological Association, accessed May 12, 2024, https://www.apa.org/news/press/releases/stress/2023/collective-trauma-recovery#:~:text).

22. Ingrid C. Chadwick and Jana L. Raver, "Not for the Faint of Heart? A Gendered Perspective on Psychological Distress in Entrepreneurship," *Journal of Occupational Health Psychology* 24, no. 6 (2019): 662–674, https://doi.org/10.1037/ocp0000157.

23. Michael T. Braun, Patrick D. Converse, and Fredrick L. Oswald, "The Accuracy of Dominance Analysis as a Metric to Assess Relative Importance: The Joint Impact of Sampling Error Variance and Measurement Unreliability," *Journal of Applied Psychology* 104, no. 4 (2019): 593–602, https://doi.org/10.1037/apl0000361.

24. "Workplace Stress," Occupational Safety and Health Administration, accessed July 10, 2024, https://www.osha.gov/workplace-stress.

25. "About Stress at Work," CDC National Institute for Occupational Safety and Health, February 13, 2024,

https://www.cdc.gov/niosh/stress/about/?CDC_AAref_Val=https://www.cdc.gov/niosh/topics/stress/default.html.

26. Emilia Bunea, "'Grace Under Pressure': How CEOs Use Serious Leisure to Cope with the Demands of Their Job," *Frontiers in Psychology* 11, no. 1453 (July 3, 2020): 1–17, https://doi.org/10.3389/fpsyg.2020.01453.

27. Psychology Today Staff, "Post-Traumatic Growth," Psychology Today, accessed May 13, 2024, https://www.psychologytoday.com/us/basics/post-traumatic-growth#:~:text.

28. George A. Bonanno, "Loss, Trauma, and Human Resilience: Have We Underestimated the Human Capacity to Thrive after Extremely Aversive Events?" *American Psychologist* 59, no. 1 (2004): 20–28, https://doi.org/10.1037/0003-066X.59.1.20.

29. Gallup, Inc., *State of the Global Workplace: 2024 Report.*

30. Aflac, *Workplace Benefits Trends: Employee Well-Being and Mental Health* (Columbus, GA: Aflac WorkForces, 2023), https://www.aflac.com/business/resources/aflac-workforces-report/default.aspx.

31. Adam Bryant, "The Leap to Leader," Harvard Business Review online, July–August 2023 issue, accessed online May 14, 2024, https://hbr.org/2023/07/the-leap-to-leader#:~:text.

32. Julia Carden, Rebecca J. Jones, and Jonathan Passmore, "Defining Self-Awareness in the Context of Adult Development: A Systematic Literature Review," *Journal of Management Education* 46, no. 1 (2021): 140–177, https://doi.org/10.1177/1052562921990065.

33. Elizabeth Perry, "Self-Awareness in Leadership: How It Will Make You a Better Boss," BetterUp, September 14, 2022, https://www.betterup.com/blog/self-awareness-in-leadership.

34. David J. Friedman, *Culture by Design: 8 Simple Steps to Drive Better Individual and Organizational Performance* (High Performing Culture, 2018), 19.

35. David J. Friedman, "Culture by Design," davidjfriedman.com, accessed May 16, 2024, https://davidjfriedman.com/.

36. Cian O Morain and Peter Aykens, "Employees Are Losing Patience with Change Initiatives," Harvard Business Review online, May 9, 2023, https://hbr.org/2023/05/employees-are-losing-patience-with-change-initiatives.

37. Bill Burnett and David Evans, *Designing Your Life: How to Build a Well-Lived, Joyful Life* (Knopf, 2016).

38. Katya Matusevich, "Developing People with the Brain in Mind: What Can TD Practitioners Learn from Neuroscience to Drive Better Results in Organizations," (In-person presentation, Barry University, Gato Gallery, Miami Shores, FL, May 14, 2019), https://www.atdsfl.org/event-3360183.

39. Taishi Kawamoto, Hiroshi Nittono, and Mitsuhiro Ura, "Cognitive, Affective, and Motivational Changes during Ostracism: An ERP, EMG, and EEG Study Using a Computerized Cyberball Task," *Journal of Neuroscience* 2013, no. 304674: 1–11, https://www.doi.org/10.1155/2013/304674.

40. Naomi I. Eisenberger et al., "An Experimental Study of Shared Sensitivity to Physical Pain and Social

Rejection," *Pain* 126, no. 1 (2006): 132–138, https://doi.org/10.1016/j.pain.2006.06.024.

41. Jean M. Twenge and Roy F. Baumeister, "Social Exclusion Increases Aggression and Self-Defeating Behavior while Reducing Intelligent Thought and Prosocial Behavior," in *The Social Psychology of Inclusion and Exclusion*, eds. D. Abrams, M. A. Hogg, and J. M. Marques (Psychology Press, 2005), 27–46.

42. Julianne Holt-Lunstad, Timothy B. Smith, and J. Bradley Layton, "Social Relationships and Mortality Risk: A Meta-analytic Review," *PLOS Medicine* 7, no. 7 (2010): e1000316. https://doi.org/10.1371/journal.pmed.1000316.

43. "The Cost of Stress," The American Institute of Stress, accessed September 2, 2024, https://www.stress.org/workplace-stress/#:~:text.

44. Gallup, Inc., *State of the Global Workplace: 2024 Report*.

45. "Good Days at Work—How Common Are They and What Causes Them?," Woohoo inc., accessed May 17, 2024, https://woohooinc.com/study-good-work-days/.

46. "The Benefits of Employee Engagement," Gallup, last modified January 7, 2023, https://www.gallup.com/workplace/236927/employee-engagement-drives-growth.aspx.

47. Sue Kraus and Sharon Sears, "Measuring the Immeasurables: Development and Initial Validation of the Self-Other Four Immeasurables (SOFI) Scale Based on Buddhist Teachings on Loving Kindness, Compassion, Joy, and Equanimity," *Social Indicators Research* 92, no. 1 (2009): 169–181, https://doi.org/10.1007/s11205-008-9300-1; Tim Lomas et

al., "Third Wave Positive Psychology: Broadening Towards Complexity," *Journal of Positive Psychology* 16, no. 5 (2021): 660–674, https://doi.org/10.1080/17439760.2020.1805501.

48. Soila Karreinen et al., "Living Through Uncertainty: A Qualitative Study on Leadership and Resilience in Primary Healthcare During COVID-19," *BMC Health Services Research* 23, no. 233 (2023): 1–13, https://doi.org/10.1186/s12913-023-09223-y.

49. Nina Hiebel et al., "Resilience in Adult Health Science Revisited—A Narrative Review Synthesis of Process-Oriented Approaches," *Frontiers in Psychology* 12, no. 659395 (2021): 1–17, https://doi.org/10.3389/fpsyg.2021.659395.

50. Paul J. Zak, "The Neuroscience of Trust: Management Behaviors that Foster Employee Engagement," Harvard Business Review online, accessed May 18, 2024, https://hbr.org/2017/01/the-neuroscience-of-trust.

51. Tom Ziglar, "You Don't Build a Business," Ziglar.com, accessed May 19, 2024, https://www.ziglar.com/articles/dont-build-business/.

52. Kevin Cope, "What is Business Acumen?," Acumen Learning, May 4, 2021, https://www.acumenlearning.com/post/what-is-business-acumen.

53. David J. Friedman, *Culture by Design: 8 Simple Steps to Drive Better Individual and Organizational Performance* (High Performing Culture, 2018).

BIBLIOGRAPHY

Aaker, Jennifer and Naomi Bagdonas. "How to Be Funny at Work." Harvard Business Review. February 5, 2021. https://hbr.org/2021/02/how-to-be-funny-at-work?utm_campaign=hbr&utm_medium=social&utm_source=linkedin.

Aflac. *Workplace Benefits Trends: Employee Well-Being and Mental Health.* Aflac WorkForces, 2023. https://www.aflac.com/business/resources/aflac-workforces-report/default.aspx.

American Psychological Association. "Stress in America 2023: A Nation Recovering from Collective Trauma." Accessed May 12, 2024. https://www.apa.org/news/press/releases/stress/2023/collective-trauma-recovery#:~:text).

Bonanno, George A. "Loss, Trauma, and Human Resilience: Have We Underestimated the Human Capacity to Thrive after Extremely Aversive Events?" *American Psychologist* 59, no. 1 (2004): 20–28. https://doi.org/10.1037/0003-066X.59.1.20.

Braun, Michael T., Patrick D. Converse, and Fredrick L. Oswald. "The Accuracy of Dominance Analysis as a Metric to

Assess Relative Importance: The Joint Impact of Sampling Error Variance and Measurement Unreliability." *Journal of Applied Psychology* 104, no. 4 (2019): 593–602. https://doi.org/10.1037/apl0000361.

Bryant, Adam. "The Leap to Leader." Harvard Business Review. July–August 2023 issue. Accessed online May 14, 2024. https://hbr.org/2023/07/the-leap-to-leader#:~:text.

Bunea, Emilia. "'Grace Under Pressure': How CEOs Use Serious Leisure to Cope with the Demands of Their Job." *Frontiers in Psychology* 11, no. 1453 (July 3, 2020): 1–17. https://doi.org/10.3389/fpsyg.2020.01453.

Burnett, Bill and David Evans. *Designing Your Life: How to Build a Well-Lived, Joyful Life*. Knopf, 2016.

Calm. "What Is Burnout? 22 Signs You're Facing It (and How to Recover)." Accessed June 23, 2024. https://www.calm.com/blog/beat-burnout.

Carden, Julia, Rebecca J. Jones, and Jonathan Passmore. "Defining Self-Awareness in the Context of Adult Development: A Systematic Literature Review." *Journal of Management Education* 46, no. 1 (2021): 140–177. https://doi.org/10.1177/1052562921990065.

Carter, Kelly and Anne Hawkins. "Joy at Work: Creating a Culture of Resilience." *Journal of Nursing Management* 50, no. 12 (2019): 34–42. https://doi,org/10.1097/01.NUMA.0000605156.88187.77.

Cassileth, Barrie R. "Complementary Therapies in Cancer Care: Humor Therapy." CancerConnect. July 27, 2018. https://news.cancerconnect.com/treatment-care/com-

plementary-therapies-in-cancer-care-humor-therapy;
Pérez-Aranda, Adrián, Jennifer Hofmann, Albert Feliu-
Soler, Carmen Ramírez-Maestre, Laura Andrés-Rodrí-
guez, Willibald Ruch, and Juan V. Luciano. "Laughing
Away the Pain: A Narrative Review of Humour, Sense
of Humour and Pain." *European Journal of Pain* 23, no. 2
(2019): 220–233. https://doi.org/10.1002/ejp.1309.

CDC National Institute for Occupational Safety and Health. "
About Stress at Work." February 13, 2024. https://www.
cdc.gov/niosh/stress/about/?CDC_AAref_Val=https://
www.cdc.gov/niosh/topics/stress/default.html.

Chadwick, Ingrid C. and Jana L. Raver. "Not for the Faint
of Heart? A Gendered Perspective on Psychological
Distress in Entrepreneurship." *Journal of Occupational
Health Psychology* 24, no. 6 (2019): 662–674. https://doi.
org/10.1037/ocp0000157.

Cope, Kevin. "What is Business Acumen?" Acumen Learning.
May 4, 2021. https://www.acumenlearning.com/post/
what-is-business-acumen.

Eisenberger, Naomi I., Johanna M. Jarcho, Matthew D. Lieber-
man, and Bruce D. Naliboff. "An Experimental Study
of Shared Sensitivity to Physical Pain and Social Rejection." *Pain* 126, no. 1 (2006): 132–138. https://doi.
org/10.1016/j.pain.2006.06.024.

Fredrickson, Barbara L. "The Role of Positive Emotions in
Positive Psychology: The Broaden-and-Build Theory of
Positive Emotions." *American Psychologist* 56, no. 3 (2001):
218–226. https://doi.org/10.1037//0003-066x.56.3.218.

Friedman, David J. "Culture by Design." Davidjfriedman.com.
Accessed May 16, 2024. https://davidjfriedman.com/.

Friedman, David J. *Culture by Design: 8 Simple Steps to Drive Better Individual and Organizational Performance*. High Performing Culture, 2018.

Gallup, Inc. *State of the Global Workplace: 2024 Report*. Gallup, Inc., 2024. https://www.gallup.com/workplace/282659/employee-burnout-perspective-paper.aspx.

Gallup. "The Benefits of Employee Engagement." Last modified January 7, 2023. https://www.gallup.com/workplace/236927/employee-engagement-drives-growth.aspx.

Hiebel, Nina, Milena Rabe, Katja Maus, Frank Peusquens, Lukas Radbruch, and Franziska Geiser. "Resilience in Adult Health Science Revisited—A Narrative Review Synthesis of Process-Oriented Approaches." *Frontiers in Psychology* 12, no. 659395 (2021): 1–17. https://doi.org/10.3389/fpsyg.2021.659395.

Holt-Lunstad, Julianne, Timothy B. Smith, and J. Bradley Layton. "Social Relationships and Mortality Risk: A Meta-analytic Review." *PLOS Medicine* 7, no. 7 (2010): e1000316. https://doi.org/10.1371/journal.pmed.1000316.

Karreinen, Soila, Henna Paananen, Laura Kihlström, Kristiina Janhonen, Moona Huhtakangas, Marjaana Viita-aho, and Liina-Kaisa Tynkkynen. "Living Through Uncertainty: A Qualitative Study on Leadership and Resilience in Primary Healthcare During COVID-19." *BMC Health Services Research* 23, no. 233 (2023): 1–13. https://doi.org/10.1186/s12913-023-09223-y.

Kawamoto, Taishi, Hiroshi Nittono, and Mitsuhiro Ura. "Cognitive, Affective, and Motivational Changes during Ostracism: An ERP, EMG, and EEG Study Using a Computerized Cyberball Task." *Journal of Neuroscience* 2013, no. 304674: 1–11. https://www.doi.org/10.1155/2013/304674.

Kraus, Sue and Sharon Sears. "Measuring the Immeasurables: Development and Initial Validation of the Self-Other Four Immeasurables (SOFI) Scale Based on Buddhist Teachings on Loving Kindness, Compassion, Joy, and Equanimity." *Social Indicators Research* 92, no. 1 (2009): 169–181. https://doi.org/10.1007/s11205-008-9300-1; Lomas, Tim, Lea Waters, Paige Williams, Lindsay G. Oades, and Margaret L. Kern. "Third Wave Positive Psychology: Broadening Towards Complexity." *Journal of Positive Psychology* 16, no. 5 (2021): 660–674. https://doi.org/10.1080/17439760.2020.1805501.

Liuba. "Joy vs Happiness: Their Differences and Impacts on Our Lives." Psychology. Accessed July 30, 2024. https://psychology.tips/joy-vs-happiness/.

Rossi, Liza. "How to Teach: SEC Cleansing & Merkaba Activators Recordings - Step 1." Love Energy Techniques. January 6–8, 2024. Lucca, Italy, Villa Il Tiglio. Unpublished presentation.

Matusevich, Katya. "Developing People with the Brain in Mind: What Can TD Practitioners Learn from Neuroscience to Drive Better Results in Organizations." In-person presentation. Barry University, Gato Gallery, Miami Shores, FL. May 14, 2019. https://www.atdsfl.org/event-3360183.

Mayo Clinic Staff. "Stress Relief from Laughter? It's No Joke." Mayo Clinic. September 22, 2023. https://www.mayoclinic.org/healthy-lifestyle/stress-management/indepth/stress-relief/art-20044456.

McPhillips, Deidre. "90% of US Adults Say the United States Is Experiencing a Mental Health Crisis, CNN/KFF Poll Finds." CNN Health. Last modified October 5, 2022. https://www.cnn.com/2022/10/05/health/cnn-kff-mental-health-poll-wellness/index.html.

Mental Health America. "Create Joy and Satisfaction." Accessed June 22, 2024. https://www.mhanational.org/create-joy-and-satisfaction#:~:text.

NLI Staff. "The Neuroscience of Laughter, and How to Inspire More of It at Work." NeuroLeadership Institute. September 17, 2020. https://neuroleadership.com/your-brain-at-work/neuroscience-laughter-at-work/; Yim, JongEun. "Therapeutic Benefits of Laughter in Mental Health: A Theoretical Review." *Tohoku Journal of Experimental Medicine* 239, no. 3 (2016): 243–249. https://doi.org/10.1620/tjem.239.243.

O Morain, Cian and Peter Aykens. "Employees Are Losing Patience with Change Initiatives." Harvard Business Review online. May 9, 2023. https://hbr.org/2023/05/employees-are-losing-patience-with-change-initiatives.

Occupational Safety and Health Administration. "Workplace Stress." Accessed July 10, 2024. https://www.osha.gov/workplace-stress.

O'Quin, Karen and Joel Aronoff. "Humor as a Technique of Social Influence." *Social Psychology Quarterly* 44, no. 4 (1981): 349–357. https://doi.org/10.2307/3033903.

Perry, Elizabeth. "Acute Stress: What You Need to Know." BetterUp. February 29, 2024. https://www.betterup.com/blog/acute-stress.

Perry, Elizabeth. "Self-Awareness in Leadership: How It Will Make You a Better Boss." BetterUp. September 14, 2022. https://www.betterup.com/blog/self-awareness-in-leadership.

Positively Present. "Stress Might Look Like . . ." Accessed May 12, 2024. https://positivelypresent.com/2014/09/23-ways-to-relax.html.

Psychology Today Staff. "Post-Traumatic Growth." Psychology Today. Accessed May 13, 2024. https://www.psychologytoday.com/us/basics/post-traumatic-growth#:~:text.

Schneiderman, Neil, Gail Ironson, and Scott D. Siegel. "Stress and Health: Psychological, Behavioral, and Biological Determinants." *Annual Review of Clinical Psychology* 1, no. 1 (2005): 607–628. https://doi.org/10.1146/annurev.clinpsy.1.102803.144141.

Stillman, Jessica. "A Huge New Study Reveals Most of Us Are Terrible at Choosing How We Spend Our Free Time." *Inc.* May 19, 2022. https://www.inc.com/jessica-stillman/happiness-satisfaction-work-life-balance-leisure-activities.html.

The American Institute of Stress. "The Cost of Stress." Accessed September 2, 2024. https://www.stress.org/workplace-stress/#:~:text.

The Providence Heart & Vascular Team. "Amazing Ways Laughter Improves Your Heart Health." Providence.

Accessed June 22, 2024. https://blog.providence.org/toyourhealthblogs/amazing-ways-laughter-improves-your-heart-health.

Twenge, Jean M. and Roy F. Baumeister. "Social Exclusion Increases Aggression and Self-Defeating Behavior while Reducing Intelligent Thought and Prosocial Behavior." In *The Social Psychology of Inclusion and Exclusion*, edited by D. Abrams, M. A. Hogg, and J. M. Marques. Psychology Press, 2005.

Vogt, Eric E., Juanita Brown, and David Isaacs. *The Art of Powerful Questions: Catalyzing Insight, Innovation, and Action*. Whole Systems Associates, 2003.

White House, The. "FACT SHEET: Biden-Harris Administration Highlights Strategy to Address the National Mental Health Crisis." May 31, 2022. https://www.whitehouse.gov/briefing-room/statements-releases/2022/05/31/fact-sheet-biden-harris-administration-highlights-strategy-to-address-the-national-mental-health-crisis/.

Woohoo inc. "Good Days at Work—How Common Are They and What Causes Them?" Accessed May 17, 2024. https://woohooinc.com/study-good-work-days/.

World Health Organization. "Burnout an 'Occupational Phenomenon': International Classification of Diseases." Last modified May 28, 2019. https://www.who.int/news/item/28-05-2019-burn-out-an-occupational-phenomenon-international-classification-of-diseases.

Zak, Paul J. "The Neuroscience of Trust: Management Behaviors that Foster Employee Engagement." Harvard Business

Review online. Accessed May 18, 2024. https://hbr. org/2017/01/the-neuroscience-of-trust.

Zetlin, Minda. "7 Small Joys You Should Make Sure to Add to Your Daily Routine in 2022." *Inc.* January 1, 2022. https://www.inc.com/minda-zetlin/2022-plans-goals-small-joys-daily-routine-happiness-productivity.html.

Ziglar, Tom. "You Don't Build a Business." Ziglar.com. Accessed May 19, 2024. https://www.ziglar.com/articles/dont-build-business/.

ABOUT THE AUTHOR

Nicole Van Valen, MS, LMFT, SHRM-SCP, is a distinguished leader, advisor, board member, and professional speaker with over two decades of experience in healthcare, behavioral health, and the entertainment industry. As a senior business leader and licensed behavioral health clinician, she enhances leadership, fosters team resilience, and promotes inclusion and belonging.

As CEO and founder of Keane Insights, Van Valen has been at the forefront of driving growth and fostering vibrant cultures within social service and healthcare organizations throughout the last decade. Her leadership has led to significant organizational transformations marked by improved team dynamics and strategic advancements. In addition to helping organizations strengthen their organizational leadership, she also offers personal development through spiritual healing and love energy techniques that enhance the holistic well-being of individuals. As a licensed mental health therapist and natural connector, she contributes to organizations through her resilience-building platform, influencing audiences around the world with thought leadership about navigating setbacks, pushing through adversity, and enhancing well-being.

Van Valen's academic background includes a Bachelor of Arts in Psychology from the University of Miami and a Master of Science in Marriage and Family Therapy from Nova Southeastern University. Following her studies, she became a licensed behavioral health clinician through the Department of Health's Division of Medical Quality Assurance to enhance her expertise in therapeutic practices. She is recognized as a Qualified Supervisor for Marriage and Family Therapy and Mental Health Counseling. Her professional depth is further highlighted by her continued studies in organizational leadership with a specialization in human resources. This is complemented by her credentials as a senior certified professional and her specialty in inclusive workplace culture and AI + HI (Artificial Intelligence + Human Interaction) from the Society for Human Resource Management, which effectively integrates her knowledge of psychology with advanced organizational dynamics and inclusive leadership principles.

Originally from the Bahamas and now residing in South Florida, Van Valen enjoys a fulfilling personal life as a wife and a mother. Her exceptional ability to navigate complex challenges and forge meaningful connections has made her a pivotal figure in empowering individuals and organizations to flourish. Her leadership style, deeply rooted in empathy and effectiveness, not only shapes organizational cultures but also enriches them with love, joy, and spirit. Van Valen's approach is transformative, fostering environments where both individuals and organizations can thrive and grow.

The B Corp Movement

Dear reader,

Thank you for reading this book and joining the Publish Your Purpose community! You are joining a special group of people who aim to make the world a better place.

What's Publish Your Purpose About?

Our mission is to elevate the voices often excluded from traditional publishing. We intentionally seek out authors and storytellers with diverse backgrounds, life experiences, and unique perspectives to publish books that will make an impact in the world.

Beyond our books, we are focused on tangible, action-based change. As a woman- and LGBTQ+-owned company, we are committed to reducing inequality, lowering levels of poverty, creating a healthier environment, building stronger communities, and creating high-quality jobs with dignity and purpose.

As a Certified B Corporation, we use business as a force for good. We join a community of mission-driven companies building a more equitable, inclusive, and sustainable global economy. B Corporations must meet high standards of transparency, social and environmental performance, and accountability as determined by the nonprofit B Lab. The certification process is rigorous and ongoing (with a recertification requirement every three years).

How Do We Do This?

We intentionally partner with socially and economically disadvantaged businesses that meet our sustainability goals. We embrace and encourage our authors and employee's differences in race, age, color, disability, ethnicity, family or marital status, gender identity or expression, language, national origin, physical and mental ability, political affiliation, religion, sexual orientation, socio-economic status, veteran status, and other characteristics that make them unique.

Community is at the heart of everything we do—from our writing and publishing programs to contributing to social enterprise nonprofits like reSET (www.resetco.org) and our work in founding B Local Connecticut.

We are endlessly grateful to our authors, readers, and local community for being the driving force behind the equitable and sustainable world we are building together.

To connect with us online or publish with us, visit us at www.publishyourpurpose.com.

Elevating Your Voice,

Jenn T Grace

Jenn T. Grace
Founder, Publish Your Purpose